The New York Times

PUBLIC PROFILES

Adolf Hitler

THE NEW YORK TIMES EDITORIAL STAFF

Published in 2019 by New York Times Educational Publishing in association with The Rosen Publishing Group, Inc. 29 East 21st Street, New York, NY 10010

First Edition

The New York Times
Alex Ward: Editorial Director, Book Development
Brenda Hutchings: Senior Photo Editor/Art Buyer
Heidi Giovine: Administrative Manager
Phyllis Collazo: Photo Rights/Permissions Editor

Rosen Publishing
Greg Tucker: Creative Director
Brian Garvey: Art Director
Megan Kellerman: Managing Editor
Jacob R. Steinberg: Editor

Cataloging-in-Publication Data
Names: New York Times Company.
Title: Adolf Hitler / edited by the New York Times editorial staff.
Description: New York : The New York Times Educational Publishing, 2019. | Series: Public profiles | Includes glossary and index.
Identifiers: ISBN 9781642820058 (pbk.) | ISBN 9781642820041 (library bound) | ISBN 9781642820034 (ebook)
Subjects: LCSH: Hitler, Adolf, 1889-1945—Juvenile literature. | Dictators—Germany—Biography—Juvenile literature. | Holocaust, Jewish (1939-1945)—Juvenile literature. | Germany—Politics and government—1933-1945—Juvenile literature.
Classification: LCC DD247.H5 A365 2019 | DDC 943.086092—dc23

Manufactured in the United States of America

On the cover: Adolf Hitler consecrating the flags of the National Socialists at the Brunswick Rally on October 11, 1931; Times Wide World Photos, Berlin Bureau.

Contents

CHAPTER 4

Hitler at War

CHAPTER 5

Hitler's Decline

CHAPTER 6

The Fuehrer's Death and Legacy

Introduction

ON JUNE 28, 1919, delegates from a war-torn, defeated Germany arrived in Versailles, France, to sign a peace treaty with the Allied forces. The Treaty of Versailles was controversial, primarily because of a specific clause, Article 231, which ascribed full blame for "the loss and damage" caused by World War I on Germany. Furthermore, demanding war reparations to the tune of 132 billion marks were to be repaid — a cost far too high for an economically devastated country still subject to a blockade in place since the start of the war.

The treaty caused outrage among Germans of every political affiliation, so much so that the first democratically elected German chancellor, Philipp Scheidemann, resigned rather than sign. However, facing the threat of a continued Allied invasion, which the German army knew that it could not hold off, the new government capitulated, and the German National Assembly voted to sign.

On June 29, a New York Times front-page story titled "Peace" hailed the signing of the treaty as "one of the greatest events in history." However, the terms of the treaty proved immediately problematic. The German economy was weak, and to keep up with the payments, the new Weimar Republic increased its printing of marks, causing hyperinflation. The Allied powers controlled imports, and most Germans could not afford basic goods, including sufficient food. Political instability led to the rise of various political factions with paramilitary forces, and coup attempts became common.

In the midst of such political upheaval, a new and captivating figure emerged, promising the German people a return to the financial prosperity, political order and national pride they felt before World War I. His name was Adolf Hitler.

Perhaps an unlikely savior figure for the Germans — he was an Austrian expatriate who moved to Bavaria after being rejected from the Academy of Fine Arts in Vienna — Hitler put forth an unabashedly nationalist platform based on extreme anti-Semitism, anti-communism, German rearmament, the annulment of the Treaty of Versailles, and the promise to restore Germany as a dominant political force in European and world politics.

Few realized just how seriously to take this rising idol, especially after his first attempted coup in 1923 failed and led to a jail sentence. In a spectacular underestimation of his will, Bavarian authorities released Hitler from prison early, deeming him "tamed." But his fiery oratory and organizational skills lay in wait. And in 1930, his National Socialist Party won big in the parliamentary elections. From then it was a rapid fall into dictatorship, military aggression against Germany's neighbors, and an unprecedented effort to exterminate Europe's Jewish population: the Holocaust.

Adolf Hitler, after having reviewed the massed legions of his Nazis, leaves the field at Nuremberg after a party assembly in 1933.

As the rest of the world watched with a combination of disbelief and horror, anti-Semitism evolved from a line item on the Nazi Party's platform to a day-to-day reality in Germany and the nations it invaded. Under Hitler's command, an estimated six million Jews, as well as millions of others including Roma, Sinti, Serbs, homosexuals and individuals with disabilities, perished in concentration camps.

In an April 8, 1945, article titled "Nazi Death Factory Shocks Germans on a Forced Tour," Gene Currivan described the conditions of the Buchenwald concentration camp as "cruelty raised to a fine art." He wrote:

> It had its gallows, torture rooms, dissection rooms, modern crematoria, laboratories where fiendish experiments were made on living human beings and its sections where people were systematically starved to death.

He described displays of "parchment" that, in reality, were framed sections of tattooed human skin as well as lamp shades made of prisoners' skin and "human skeletons who had lost all likeness to anything human."

These atrocities far exceeded what the world suspected was happening to German Jews. Buchenwald was just one of more than 40,000 concentration camps established by the Nazis before and during World War II. They represent the most cruel manifestation of Hitler's vision for Europe: a land for the Germans where other ethnic groups had no right to live.

By committing suicide ahead of the Soviet capture of Berlin, Hitler escaped the post-war Nuremberg Trials, where his cohorts were held responsible for these war crimes. Nonetheless, these articles offer a different trial: They document in real time the rise and fall of one of history's greatest villains — including voices of condemnation and premature dismissals, horrified reproaches and belated realizations, his destructive successes and ultimate demise. They stand as testimony to what an extreme nationalist movement looks like as it unfolds and the risks it poses to basic decency and human rights.

CHAPTER 1

The Rise of a Menace

On Nov. 21, 1922, Adolf Hitler's name first appeared in The New York Times in a profile noting his strong oratorical skills and ability to rally the average German behind a nationalistic message disparaging Jews and communists, and promising economic prosperity to post-war Germany. One year later, The Times covered the famous Beer Hall Putsch in Munich and Hitler's subsequent trial, imprisonment and release. In 1924, the German government believed prison had tamed Hitler and "he was no longer to be feared." These, indeed, were famous last words.

New Popular Idol Rises in Bavaria

BY CYRIL BROWN | NOV. 21, 1922

MUNICH, NOV. 20 — Next to the high cost of living and the dollar, "Der Hitler" and his "Hakenkreuzlers" are the popular topic of talk in Munich and other Bavarian towns. This reactionary Nationalistic anti-Semitic movement has now reached a point where it is considered potentially dangerous, though not for the immediate future.

Hitler today is taken seriously among all classes of Bavarians. He is feared by some, enthusiastically hailed as a prophet and political economic savior by others, and watched with increasing sympathetic interest by the bulk who, apparently, are merely biding the psychological moment to mount Hitler's bandwagon. Undoubtedly the spectacular success of Mussolini and the Fascisti brought Hitler's movement to the fore and gained popular interest and sympathy for it. Another condition favorable to the outburst of the movement is the widespread discontent with the existing state of affairs among all classes in the towns and cities under the increasing economic pressure.

Hitler's "Hakenkreuz" movement is essentially urban in character. It has not yet caught a foothold among the hardy Bavarian peasantry and highlanders, which would make it really dangerous. As a highly placed personage put it:

Hitler organized a small insignificant group of National Socialists two years ago, since when the movement has been smoldering beneath the surface. Now it has eaten its way through, and a conflagration of course is not only possible but certain if this now free flame of fanatical patriotism finds sufficient popular combustible material to feed on.

Hitler has been called the Bavarian Mussolini, and his followers the Bavarian Fascisti. There is nothing socialistic about the National Socialism he preaches. He has 30,000 organized followers in Munich alone. His total following throughout Bavaria is uncertain, since the movement is in a state of rapid flux. He is wasting no time working out political programs, but devotes his whole energy to recruiting fresh forces and perfecting his organization.

BLACKJACKS SILENCE OPPOSITION

"Herr Hitler regrets he is unable to meet you as he is leaving town on important business for several days," was the answer received by The New York Times correspondent. His important business was going to Regensburg with three special trainloads of Munich admirers for the purpose of holding a series of reactionary inflammatory meetings and incidentally to beat up protesting Socialists and Communists with blackjacks if any dare protest, which is becoming increasingly rarer.

His simple method is, first, propaganda and secondly, efficient organization. He personally conducts patriotic revival meetings for this purpose, often descending from his stronghold Munich, on other Bavarian towns with special trainloads of followers. He has the rare oratorical gift, at present unique in Germany, of spellbinding whole audiences regardless of politics or creed. The new converts made at these rallies, those who absolutely and unconditionally pledge themselves to Hitler and the cause, are carefully sifted through and the pick of them who pass the standard military muster are organized into "storm troops" with gray shirts, brassards in the old imperial colors, black and an anti-Semitic Swastika cross in a white circular field on red; armed also with blackjacks and, it is popularly whispered, revolvers.

According to a reliable specialist informant, there are probably 400,000 military rifles and 150 cannon still concealed in Bavaria. So that some fine day Hitler's legionaries might well make their debut with rifles.

Hitler's strength is in the combination of his undeniable great gifts as an orator and organizer. He exerts an uncanny control over audiences, possessing the remarkable ability to not only rouse his hearers to a fighting pitch of fury, but at will to turn right around and reduce the same audience to docile calmness and good order. A typical instance is related by the informant mentioned:

> At the height of the recent Bavarian Government crisis Hitler was holding a mass meeting in Munich and had worked up the big audience when a rumor spread through the hall that he had planned a coup and that he would overthrow and seize the Government that night and was about to give the signal at this rally. His followers burst into an enthusiastic uproar, drew and brandished blackjacks and revolvers, and with shouts of "Heil, Heil, Heil" prepared to follow Hitler and storm anything.
>
> With a few electric words he worked a magic change in the audience. Their duty, on which the success of the cause depended, he said, was iron discipline and implicit obedience to orders when orders were given. The time for action had not come yet. And the riot was, pipped in the bud.

A DIFFERENT SHOW OF POWER

A different exhibition of Hitler power: During a mass meeting in Nuremberg, a stronghold of Bavarian socialism, the radical elements undertook a counter-demonstration, massed outside the meeting hall and sang the "Internationale." The strains of the hated tune heard in the hall enraged Hitler's followers. At his word of command shock troops of gray shirts with fine discipline marched from the hall, pulled their blackjacks, charged and dispersed the crowd with many a broken head.

Hitler is credited with having a rapidly increasing following among the workers disgruntled by the high cost of living. It is also said many ultra-radicals, including Communists, have flocked to his reactionary banner. He is beginning to draw support from the politically sluggish middle classes, which in Bavaria, however, are not so sluggish as in Berlin. Even more significant there is some active, more passive support and to a still greater extent sympathetic interest for the Hitler movement among the Bavarian loyalists, among monarchists and militarists and in government and political circles, apparently coupled with the idea that the movement would prove a useful tool if it could be controlled by their special interests. But there is also the latent fear that the movement might wax beyond control.

Hitler, in addition to his oratorical and organizing abilities, has another positive asset — he is a man of the "common people" and hence has the makings of a "popular hero," appealing to all classes. It is reported that he was a worker before becoming leader of the Bavarian Social Nationalists. He served during the war as a common soldier and won the Iron Cross of the First and Second Classes, which for a common soldier is distinctive evidence of exceptional bravery and daring. To Bavarian mentality he talks rough, shaggy, sound horse sense, and according to present Bavarian public opinion a strong, active leader equipped with horse sense is the need of the hour.

CHIEF POINTS OF HIS PROGRAM

Hitler's program is of less interest than his person and movement. His program consists chiefly of half a dozen negative ideas clothed in generalities. He is "against the Jews, Communists, Bolshevism, Marxian socialism, Separatists, the high cost of living, existing conditions, the weak Berlin Government and the Versailles Treaty." Positively he stands only for "a strong united Germany under a strong Government."

He is credibly credited with being actuated by lofty, unselfish patriotism. He probably does not know himself just what he wants to accomplish. The keynote of his propaganda in speaking and writing is violent anti-Semitism. His followers are popularly nicknamed "the Hakenkreuzler." So violent are Hitler's fulminations against the Jews that a number of prominent Jewish citizens are reported to have sought safe asylums in the Bavarian highlands, easily reached by fast motor cars, whence they could hurry their women and children when forewarned of an anti-Semitic St. Bartholomew's night.

But several reliable, well-informed sources confirmed the idea that Hitler's anti-Semitism was not so genuine or violent as it sounded, and that he was merely using anti-Semitic propaganda as a bait to catch masses of followers and keep them aroused, enthusiastic and in line for the time when his organization is perfected and sufficiently powerful to be employed effectively for political purposes.

A sophisticated politician credited Hitler with peculiar political cleverness for laying emphasis and over-emphasis on anti-Semitism, saying; "You can't expect the masses to understand or appreciate your finer real aims. You must feed the masses with cruder morsels and ideas like anti-Semitism. It would be politically all wrong to tell them the truth about where you really are leading them."

The Hitler movement is not of mere local or picturesque interest. It is bound to bring Bavaria into a renewed clash with the Berlin Government as long as the German Republic goes even through the motions of trying to live up to the Versailles Treaty. For it is certain the Allies will take umbrage at the Hitler organization as a violation of the military clauses of the treaty and demand disbandment, even as in the case of its predecessor, the Orgesch.

Bavarian Riots Continue

BY THE NEW YORK TIMES | NOV. 12, 1923

On Nov. 8, 1923, Hitler and others attempted a coup in Munich, Bavaria, in an event now known as the Beer Hall Putsch.

MUNICH, NOV. 11 — Adolph Hitler, the fugitive chief of the Bavarian Fascisti, is rallying his supporters in the Isar Valley, and his dramatic return is a possibility. Indeed, it is feared that the disorders of the last few days may be only the prelude to further and far more serious conflicts.

Reichswehr and Green Police are concentrated at the main station in view of a possible advance by Hitler's forces.

Leaflets are being posted up by cyclists of the Hitler party, stating that companies of the Reichswehr have mutinied against Dr. von Kahr's orders and that the men on duty are imported from Soviet Saxony.

That Dictator von Kahr must resign is thought almost inevitable. Ever since the defeat of the rebels on Friday demonstrations against von Kahr have continued in the streets, and the troops and police have had the greatest difficulty in maintaining order. Many of the demonstrators are obviously remnants of the Hitler storm troops, although they are careful to wear no uniform or badges.

Soon after 8 o'clock this evening a company of soldiers charged with fixed bayonets into a retreating crowd, using the butts of their rifles at close quarters. Five civilians were taken away on stretchers and there were at least eight other casualties.

CRIES OF DOWN WITH KAHR

On Friday afternoon mounted Green Police with lances were chasing small bands of cyclists who were parading the streets shouting "Down with Kahr the traitor." Since then processions and assemblies of more than three persons have been prohibited and places of amusement and restaurants must close at 8 o'clock, after which hour no one is allowed to be on the streets without a police permit. But as before indicated this has not deterred the demonstrators. Students from universities, with their professors, paraded last night shouting "Down with Kahr" and epithets such as "Judas." The procession was partly dispersed by blank shell fire.

The police and troops are behaving with admirable restraint under the greatest provocation. This morning a group of apparently respectable citizens were spitting on the Green Police, who were tactfully trying to get the crowd to move on. Accusations of cowardice and treachery in the foulest language were shouted at the unfortunate men on duty.

Most of the public squares are closed to the public with barbed wire and machine guns. It is stated that the troops, except the machine gunners, are only armed with blank cartridges, but covered steel truncheons are now being used more frequently by some soldiers whose sorely tried patience is becoming exhausted. Percy Brown of The London Daily Graphic, who was with the correspondent this morning trying to take pictures, was attacked by some Green Police and beaten with their steel truncheons.

An attempt is obviously being made to establish Hitler as a martyr. Kahr, for his part, asserts that Hitler has given his solemn oath only to act in loyal support of the Dictatorship. Disinterested spectators think there is little to choose between the two in the matter of loyalty

KAHR AND LOSSOW "EXPLAIN"

Dr. von Kahr received yesterday representatives of the press and explained to them the course events had taken in Munich from the moment when Hitler broke into the meeting in the wine cellar which Dr. von Kahr was addressing on Thursday evening and announced the Nationalist coup. Statements were also made by General von Lossow and Colonel von Sessner, who co-operated with him in suppressing the Hitler-Ludendorff movement.

How near the putsch came to success may be judged from the fact that the remnants of the Bavarian Cabinet headed by Dr. Matt,

Minister of Education, fled Friday morning to Regensburg when they issued their proclamation declaring Hitler's coup d'état an act of treason against Bavaria and the Reich at the meeting on Thursday night in the Burgerbrau cellar after Hitler had announced the composition of his new "government." He declared that the Stresemann Government would be overthrown and the National army would march on Berlin and establish a truly national government.

The first action of Hitler's dictatorship was to march a putsch, armored car and machine gun detachments to the offices of the Müncher Post, which were almost completely wrecked by the machine gun and bombs. During the night gangs of Hitlerites stormed through the town and raided the first-class restaurants and hotels in search of Jews or profiteers. Fortunately there was no bloodshed although a considerable amount of promiscuous shooting occurred.

THE DAY AFTER THE COUP

On Friday morning the correspondent drove through the town at 6 o'clock with one of Hitler's staff in a requisitioned car, one of many which the new government had taken over. The streets were filled with Hitler's men posting up proclamations. The bridges were all heavily guarded and the town appeared to be at the mercy of the Hitler forces. Some of the posters announced that military tribunals would be established to deal with looting or other crimes, and that there would be only two verdicts, not guilty or guilty, and only one penalty for the guilty — death.

Eventually we drove to the Biirgerbrauhalle, where Hitler and von Ludendorff had established their headquarters. Here the scene was reminiscent of the early days of the war. Uniforms, rations and equipment were being issued. Small youths with or without uniforms were drilling in various courtyards. Recruits were being enlisted. Everywhere the utmost enthusiasm and optimism prevailed. Outside, rows of lorries were drawn up which moved off at intervals with troops, munitions or supplies. All thought that the movement was a success.

Then news came through that the City Hall had been occupied and the Council ejected. An officer who brought the news said: "We have 160,000 perfectly equipped men and we must march under von Ludendorff to victory."

Upstairs in a small, barely furnished room where von Ludendorff and Hitler and half a dozen officers with maps and plans, Hitler received the correspondent courteously but was obviously overwrought and dead tired. He scarcely seemed to fill the part — this little man in an old waterproof coat with a revolver at his hip, unshaven and with disordered hair, and so hoarse that he could scarcely speak.

Von Ludendorff also seemed anxious and preoccupied as he talked with some Hitler political advisers. He too was extremely friendly. The Government, he said, was anxious to have the approval of England. He went on to talk of the future glory of new Germany. He also offered a pass that permitted moving about without hindrance, and also to arrange for communication with Berlin, all telephone and telegraphic communication with the outer world being completely cut off.

He rushed upstairs to fill out a form, but when he returned his manner had completely altered. The General Staff was signing no passes.

REASON FOR CHANGE OF FRONT

Arriving back in the centre of the town the reason for this sudden change was clear. During the morning in the safety of Police Headquarters, Dr. von Kahr and General von Lossow had had time to reconsider their pledges to Hitler. A proclamation signed by von Kahr appeared stating that Hitler and Ludendorff were traitors, that the consent which had been forced from von Kahr at the pistol's point was withdrawn, that the Reichswehr and Landespolizei were loyal to the von Kahr government and Hitler's forces and all similar organizations of storm troops must be dissolved forthwith.

Hitler and his advisers evidently refused to believe the game was lost. With Hitler and Ludendorff (the latter dressed in civilian clothes with a green felt hat) at their head, some 5,000 Nationalists began to march through the town. Almost simultaneously Reichswehr reinforcements arrived from the various outlying depots, and a strong detachment with an armored car and machine guns took up positions in the Odeonsplatz.

The Hitler army, many of them entirely unsuspectingly, marched past the National Opera House and in the narrow streets leading to the Odeonsplatz received the command to halt. This was followed almost immediately by rifle and machine gun fire. Hitler was wounded slightly in the arm and disappeared in a motor car, but it looked as though orders had been given that Ludendorff was not to be fired on. According to an eyewitness Ludendorff was taking no risks and threw himself flat on the paving stones. Afterward he walked up to a Reichswehr officer and was taken into custody. He was kept in a building until 10 o'clock when he was released on parole.

Hitler's men fled in all directions, many throwing away their arms.

In less than half an hour complete order was restored. The putsch had failed and von Kahr was once again supreme dictator.

The casualties numbered 18 killed and 20 wounded. Most of them were merely misguided youths who suffered for their blind faith in the extravagant promises of their political leaders.

During the fighting Reichswehr troops brought machine-guns into the garden of the British consulate, which backs up on the old war ministry where a party of Hitlerites were in hiding. In the attempt to surround the rebels three of the soldiers were wounded by Hitler snipers in the garden before superior numbers prevailed and the Ministry of war was recaptured.

Hitler Writes a Book While in Prison Cell

BY THE NEW YORK TIMES | MAY 30, 1924

BERLIN, MAY 29 — The name of Adolf Hitler, who with General Ludendorff led last Autumn's revolt against the German Republic, will soon be added to the list of political prisoners who have utilized their prison term to write books. Hitler announced that he was writing a book, when interviewed recently at the fortress in Landsberg, Bavaria, where he is serving the short sentence for treason imposed on him after, the sensational Munich trial last month.

He told the admirer interviewing him that his uprising saved Germany from a dictatorship, behind which the man pulling the strings would have been the late Hugo Stinnes, the greatest German financial magnate. According to Hitler, General von Seeckt, now Commander of the Germany Army, was to head this dictatorship, together with Herr Minoux, a prominent coadjutor of Stinnes in his manifold business enterprises. The immediate result, said Hitler, would have been that the German railways would have been pawned to foreigners. The only salvation for Germany, Hitler continued, was a Voelkisch dictatorship, which he predicted was sure to come.

At Landsberg the interviewer found postcards on sale everywhere with Hitler's picture and evidence of the prisoner's immense popularity among the inhabitants. This admirer calls Hitler a "man who some day will be reckoned among the greatest of his people."

Hitler Tamed by Prison

BY THE NEW YORK TIMES | **DEC. 21, 1924**

BERLIN, DEC. 20 — Adolph Hitler, once the demigod of the reactionary extremists, was released on parole from imprisonment at Fortress Landsberg, Bavaria, today and immediately left in an auto for Munich. He looked a much sadder and wiser man today than last Spring when he, with Ludendorff and other radical extremists, appeared before a Munich court charged with conspiracy to overthrow the Government.

His behavior during imprisonment convinced the authorities that, like his political organization, known as the Völkischer, he was no longer to be feared. It is believed he will retire to private life and return to Austria, the country of his birth.

DPA DENA/PICTURE-ALLIANCE/DPA/AP IMAGES

Hitler outside Landsberg Prison on the day of his release, Dec. 20, 1924. He served just over one year of his five-year sentence for treason.

CHAPTER 2

Fascism, and Hitler, Gains Followers

Following release from prison, Hitler faced a new Germany in which the economy had improved and politics had become less divisive. He was barred from giving public speeches in Bavaria — a ban that lasted until 1927 — but his associates helped spread the National Socialist platform while Hitler quietly awaited his own return to the spotlight. When the German economy crashed in 1929, conditions were ripe for Hitler's party to make gains, and in 1930, the Nazis won 107 of 577 seats in the Reichstag — an increase from 12 seats in the previous election.

Fascists Make Big Gains in Germany

BY GUIDO ENDERIS | SEPT. 15, 1930

THE SENSATIONAL GAINS of Adolph Hitler's National Socialist-Labor or Fascist party in yesterday's election constitutes one of the most upsetting developments of German post-war politics and, while predictions conceded it a five-fold increase over its previous Reichstag delegation, its vote of more than 6,000,000 and capture of 100 and more seats can be explained by the adroit manner in which it exploited the post-war social and economic privations of the middle classes and such working classes as are not followers of the Socialists or Communists.

Herr Hitler also kindled the imagination of millions of young voters by the fiery nature of his oratory, while the more mature electorate was fed with anti-Semitic, anti-reparations and anti-parliamentary haranguing. Back of it all was the cry for a dictator who would lead Germany out of the slough of parliamentary despond.

Herr Hitler's meetings boasted the largest attendance of those of any party and his organization apparently was liberally financed, the assumption being that various big industrialists preferred to see the proletariat mobilized under the Fascist flag rather than under the red standard of Moscow.

As the political programs of Herren Hitler and Hugenberg agree on such cardinal points as opposition to reparations payments and German foreign policies, it may be assumed that the two groups will cooperate in the new Reichstag while the Communist will prove a handy ally when it comes to blocking parliamentary procedure. German reds heretofore have invariably voted with the Fascists in opposition to every government step. These three groups will now jointly command 222 seats out of a total of 577 in the new Reichstag, and it will require all the resources of a faultlessly functioning coalition of the Socialists and middle parties to protect the future of parliamentary procedure.

Of the middle parties, which heavily lost ground in yesterday's voting, the People's party, which since the death of Gustav Stresemann has been leaderless, lost 19 seats, while the newly founded State party, which expected to absorb the entire liberal vote of Germany, captured only 22 seats. It was engulfed in the wave of apathy which seized the German bourgeoisie, and which also affected the new conservative People's party, which comprised secessionists from the Hugenberg Nationalist party. Although this new group, which is headed by Captain Gottfried Treviranus, a member of the Bruening Cabinet, had 19 Deputies in the last Reichstag, its delegation was cut down to five in today's election.

Fascists Glorify Pan-German Ideal

BY THE NEW YORK TIMES | SEPT. 15, 1930

THE NATIONAL SOCIALIST PARTY, or the German Fascist party, represents the extreme Pan-German ideal of a purely German State. Its platform includes demands for the immediate unification of Germany and Austria, annulment of the treaties of Versailles and St. Germain, equality in military force with every other country in Europe, the restoration of Germany's colonies, the nationalization of all trusts, the participation of workers in the profits of manufacturing, discontinuance of reparation payments, the socialization of industry and a nationwide campaign to disfranchise or drive from Germany all the Jews.

Other planks in the party's platform, drawn up by its founder, Adolf Hitler, known as the German Mussolini, are the following:

• The land shall be nationalized without compensation and exploited for the common good.

• The death penalty shall be applied to usurers and persons who have made large profits out of their fellow men.

• All non-Germans shall be expelled from Germany as long as unemployment exists and while it is impossible properly to nourish all German citizens.

• No further immigration of non-Germans shall be permitted and all non-Germans who have entered Germany since Aug. 2, 1914, shall be immediately expelled.

• The first duty of every citizen is to be physically and mentally at work; those who do not work shall not eat.

• Unearned income is to be abolished.

• All department stores shall be confiscated by the State, divided into small shops and rented at nominal prices to small shopkeepers.

• The State shall purchase its supplies mainly from small shopkeepers.

- The Reichswehr shall be dissolved and a large national army established.

- All journalists must be German citizens, and all productions of art and literature contrary to the principles of true Germanism are to be suppressed.

PROGRAM WIDELY DISTRIBUTED

This program was distributed by the millions throughout Germany during the present campaign.

Herr Hitler, a one-time architectural draftsman, is, ironically enough, a man without a country. Born in Braunau on the Inn, in upper Austria, on April 20, 1889, he lost his Austrian citizenship when he volunteered in the German army at the outbreak of the war. He failed to apply for German citizenship when he was still a political non-entity, and since he has become the avowed enemy of the present republican form of government his applications for citizenship have been constantly rejected.

On Nov. 8, 1923, Herr Hitler, along with General von Ludendorff, staged the notorious Bavarian "Putsch" to overthrow the government, declaring himself dictator of Germany. The revolt was quelled the following day and next April Herr Hitler was sentenced to five years' imprisonment. He spent a year in prison, during which time his party deserted him. No longer considered a menace the Government took pity on him and released him.

As the Fascist party in Italy is the creation of Benito Mussolini, so is the Fascist party in Germany the creation of Adolf Hitler. His chief power lies in his oratory and he is ranked in this respect with Alexander Kerensky, Leon Trotsky, Aristide Briand and Signor Mussolini. So dangerous was his oratory considered by the authorities that for four years he was forbidden by every State in Germany, with the exception of Thuringia and Mecklenburg, to speak in public. The ban was first lifted by Bavaria in 1927, but Prussia did not lift it until this year.

Herr Hitler's sonorous, penetrating tenor, combined with his histrionic ability, makes him especially effective with audiences of young men and young women, the backbone of his party. He is also regarded as a remarkable organizer.

A REMARKABLE COME-BACK

Herr Hitler's comeback after the total collapse of his "Putsch" is considered one of the most remarkable in modern European politics. For a time after the collapse he had hardly a friend left. During his year in prison his party united, against his express command, with the German People's Freedom party. One month after his release he had won enough disciples to found his present party and, in the Reichstag elections of May 1928, he polled a vote of 809,541, gaining 12 mandates to Parliament.

In their method and organization the German Fascists very closely resemble the Communists. One of the most effective instruments organized by Herr Hitler is the "storm squads," duplicates of the Communist "red front squads." These "storm squads" are thoroughly trained with weapons and are excellently equipped for street fighting with the Communists. The two parties have been held responsible for 90 percent of the political killings and street brawls that have made German post-war elections the most violent in any European country.

Hitler, Driving Force in Germany's Fascism

BY JOSEPH SHAPLEN | **SEPT. 21, 1930**

WHEN ON THE NIGHT of Nov. 9, 1923, Adolf Hitler, assisted by General Erich Ludendorff, launched his abortive revolution against Berlin in the Rathskeller of the City Hall in Munich, a Gargantuan outburst of laughter resounded throughout Germany. The "revolution" collapsed before it could get under way. Adolf Hitler became the nation's political clown.

Deserted soon thereafter even by his own followers, at odds with his chief supporter Ludendorff, and facing trial and imprisonment for conspiracy against the State, there appeared to be nothing in store for Hitler but oblivion. He was tried and sentenced to five years' imprisonment. Of this he served only one year. The German Republic, in its feeling of security and with a magnanimity not often displayed by governments toward conspirators who seek its destruction, released him, making him a present of four years of life which otherwise he would have had to spend behind the bars.

Hitler took good advantage of these four years. Today, five years after his release from prison, he stands as the leader of the second strongest political party in Germany, challenging the very life of the republic. Acknowledged leader of German youth, he is hailed by millions as the German Mussolini, come to free Germany from domestic depression and the foreign yoke. When, some time in the middle of next month, the new Reichstag chosen on Sept. 14 assembles in the gray pile facing the Platz der Republik, no less than 107 Fascists, members of the National Socialist Workers' Party — Hitler's party — will occupy seats in the legislative assembly.

SPECTACULAR RISE TO POWER

In November, 1923, Hitler counted only 200,000 followers, in the last Reichstag his Deputies numbered 12. On Sept. 14, nearly 6,500,000

Germans flocked to his support, lifting him in one day from the status of political nonentity to that of a national figure.

What is the meaning of this transformation? What are the causes behind it? One could make a long and detailed analysis of political, economic and social factors responsible for this phenomenal rise of German Fascism and with it of Adolf Hitler, but most important of all the forces responsible is Hitler himself. Whatever else the German election has proved, it has demonstrated once again the truth so frequently challenged in this era of rapidly growing collectivism — the importance of the individual in politics and in history. For just as Italian Fascism would have been impossible without Mussolini and Russian Bolshevism without Lenin, so is the movement in Germany, which on Sept. 14 announced its presence with a thundering salvo of votes, inconceivable without Hitler. Hitler is its driving power and its inspiration.

Like many other leaders of important political and social movements, Hitler is a man of the people, a carpenter by trade. Politically he is an outcast, a man without a country. Born in Austria, he enlisted in the German army at the outbreak of the war. This lost him his Austrian citizenship. After the war he failed to avail himself of the opportunity to become a citizen of Germany. When later, after he had placed himself at the head of the Fascist movement, he sought German citizenship, it was denied to him. Perhaps he may have to wait for it until he is in a position to confer it upon himself.

HE HAS ENERGY AND RESERVE

Hitler is 41. He is of medium height, wiry, slender, with dark hair, bristling, toothbrush mustache, eye spurting fire, straight nose, finely chiseled face and a delicate complexion, quite unlike the Furor Teutonicus which he is represented to be. His entire being breathes dynamic energy combined with a marked reserve. Four years in the trenches taught him to have no fear of death. He is an orator of apostolic fervor, and while the things he says are regarded by politically sensible people as pure ignorance and demagogy, he says them with a magnetism and a driving power irresistible to old and young, particularly the latter.

It is significant that most of Germany's 5,000,000 new voters in the recent election cast their votes for Hitler's party. It is to the young people, who know nothing of the war, whose hearts and minds burn with a desire to play a part in the life of their country and its future, that Hitler and his oratory make their greatest appeal.

It is very doubtful whether many can make much sense out of the inchoate mixture of ideas that constitute his program — a mixture of socialism, bolshevism, nationalism, militarism, anti-republicanism and anti-Semitism. Apparently it matters little to his followers what he says. Their chief concern seems to he how he says it. What he says may not appear true to those who know better, but to those who like it, it is not without its logic.

Perhaps the best characterization of his doctrine yet given is "national bolshevism" — "national" in the sense that he stands for the repudiation of all Germany's obligations, the tearing up of the Treaty of Versailles and a war of liberation, if need be; "bolshevist" in the sense that he claims to be the foe of that big, industrialist capitalism of Germany, which he asserts is responsible for all of Germany's woes. By combining these two elements in his program he appeals to the youth of the land as well as to that large middle class which has suffered most from the social and economic perturbations following the war and from the present depression.

The effect of Hitler's eloquence and personality has been well described by a German who attended one of his early meetings in Munich:

> I look around at my neighbors. At my left sits an old aristocrat, a General in the World War. At my right, in the working clothes of the Eastern suburbs of Munich, a man whose honest eyes alone redeem his desperate face. Only after the meeting warms up does he tell me that up to a short time ago he was a convinced Communist, and that only through Hitler has he learned to feel himself a German.

Suddenly every one jumps up and a roar of applause sweeps through the big hall. Upon the speakers' platform steps a simple, modest looking, slender man of medium height who seems underfed and overworked. He is in the later thirties. His voice certainly is not unpleasant, but neither is it exactly fascinating. Although the man seems to be in a fever of enthusiasm he remains outwardly calm and restrained.

In astonishment I note that the condescending look of the old General on my left is gradually making way for an expression of rapt attention. "What a remarkable range of knowledge and technical learning!" he whispers in my ear. And later, as the accusation of complicity in Germany's want and misery is presented with almost crushing force, "How fearfully excited the man must be, despite his external calm; he can't have a dry thread on his body!"

My neighbor on the right, the Communist, no longer merely claps his hands in applause; in his eyes I think I see tears, and at every slight pause in the speaker's address he roars approval with all his might. In fact, in spite of the speaker's moderate tone, a very hurricane of elemental passion seems to be sweeping down upon the audience.

So it is no wonder, then, that when Hitler, after having spoken two and a half hours, ends to a terrific storm of applause, the General and the Communist walk fraternally to a table to enroll as members of the National Socialist Party. Everywhere there are flashing eyes and exalted spirits. Youthful forms, although showing signs of semi-starvation, brace up proudly.

"Yes, yes, there still lives in us, thank God, a little of the old Germanism, despite all the corruption," a lady of my acquaintance calls to me as we go out. And a professor remarks, "No college instructor can excel this man in the unshakable logic of his construction or in his powers of conviction."

We are met with howls of rage from Hitler's enemies when we reach the street, but they are soon silenced by one of his patrols.

Such is the man who has announced himself as the leader of the young generation of Germany and who may or may not prove the author of a new war of revenge.

Hitler's Rhetoric

BY THE NEW YORK TIMES | SEPT. 27, 1930

IF IT BE TRUE that a watched pot never boils, the menace of Adolf Hitler has been grossly exaggerated. His speech before the Supreme Court at Leipzig was in substance an invitation to the whole world to watch him boil over. There is an innocence almost childish about the detailed fashion in which he set out to be blood-curdling. Almost one expected him to state the precise number of heads that would roll from the guillotine when the Fascists have taken over control of the German nation and inaugurated the day of reckoning. There is something which may be innocence or mere confusion of ideas about his coupling the overthrow of the German Republic, the repudiation of the peace treaties and the mobilization of the guillotine with the legal two-thirds majority required by the Weimar Constitution. People will find it another mark of the ingrained German respect for law and order that even

Hitler makes a speech during the election campaign of 1930. He is a rising political star in Germany, and oratory has proved to be his greatest tool.

revolution and massacre must pause to make sure that they are not Verboten. These are not the deprecatory half-measures employed by the original practitioners of fascism in Italy or of the Communist variety of fascism in Russia. Mussolini's or Lenin's manifestoes were concerned with programs and principles and not with the dreadful things they would do to their enemies as soon as they got ready.

To dismiss the Hitlerite rhetoric, for all its naïveté, as of no consequence would be wrong. Since 1914 no one will venture to say what dire mischief may not be let loose by infantile irresponsibility. It requires no great talent to get on the nerves of the nations in the new European order and particularly in the present economic discontent. Yet, humanly speaking, the net result of the 6,000,000 votes cast for the Hitlerite platform of dictatorship and war, the net result of that flamboyant speech at Leipzig, should be to bring together the parties and elements in Germany standing for sobriety and the existing political order. These were a majority in the Reichstag election and may be expected to show a more decisive majority if it ever comes to a showdown. Many Germans who registered their economic and social grievances by voting Fascist a fortnight ago will think twice before actually inviting civil war and the return of French troops to German soil.

Wherever in Western Europe fascism has asserted itself successfully it has come as the retort to an experiment in communism, or from fear of a foreign enemy. It is still the doctrine in Italy that Mussolini's march on Rome saved the country from Red domination and from the dark designs of certain foreign powers. In Bavaria and Hungary an actual taste of communism preceded and prepared the way for the rule of the strong hand. These seemingly necessary conditions for flinging one's self into the arms of dictatorship Germany today obviously does not fulfill. She is in no danger from her domestic proletarians. And, despite the talk of Germany's enslavement by the peace treaties the signs of her servitude are fast disappearing.

CHAPTER 3

Hitler Named Chancellor, then Fuehrer

Although the Nazi Party fared well in the 1930 election, Hitler still faced one major obstacle to consolidating his power. Born in Austria and never naturalized, he was not a German citizen and, therefore, could not hold public office. But in 1932, he was granted citizenship and became chancellor later that year. In 1933 and 1934, he gained dictatorial powers, becoming Nazi Germany's "fuehrer." Hitler's tone and actions became increasingly belligerent, as Germany gradually occupied and annexed neighboring regions and suppressed political dissidents and Jews.

Hitler Sees Fight to Finish in Reich

BY THE NEW YORK TIMES | JAN. 18, 1932

BERLIN, JAN. 17 — At a mass meeting under the auspices of the National Socialist Students' Association here tonight, Adolf Hitler delivered an ardent address in which he declared that the one hope and possibility for a truly united Germany and for her political and economic restoration lay in the victory of the National Socialist movement and the consequent acquisition by the nation of a totally different political organization.

The meeting was held on the eve of student elections and also on the eve of the sixty-first anniversary of the founding of the German Empire.

Hitler stands with members of the National Socialist Student's Association following his address to the organization on Jan. 17, 1932.

Germany had decayed nationally and politically because her leadership, splendid in science, industry and most other fields of human endeavor, had failed her miserably in matters political, Herr Hitler declared. What mattered, he added, was not whether the Bruening government or another held office but a root and branch change without which Germany's final doom was already written.

HOW HE WOULD GAIN UNITY

"It is futile for the gentlemen of the old school to clamor 'Unite, be of one mind,' for union is not going to be accomplished that way," Herr Hitler said.

> Germany is now torn into two hostile camps, Marxists against nationalists and burghers. There is no composing their opposition. If one were not to conquer the other the result won be two classes hermetically closed from each other, so that in the end they would not even be able to talk together and would speak different languages.

There is no way of bridging this opposition, and those who advocate domestic compromises and conciliations only manifest their lack of political reason, for obviously what is needed is to push the fight to the utmost until one side conquers the other and thus brings about the possibility of reuniting the now internecinely torn Germans into a new unity.

Such a unity, Herr Hitler declared, could he brought about in only one way, through organization, and there must be political leadership to weld that organization and guide the national will. The "pernicious doctrine" of "mass democracy" written in the Weimar Constitution must be abolished, he emphasized.

THE CHIEF "NAZI" ACHIEVEMENT

"What I claim as the greatest achievement of the National Socialist movement," Herr Hitler went on, "is that it has dragged from obscurity 30,000 men who now are leaders of their local groups, hundreds who have a following in large districts and scores who have a national following — and without us under the old system not one of these men would ever have been heard of.

"The people will follow leaders that are truly their own — they will follow no others. And without such leadership and rewelding of the national mind and reorganization, Germany must decline more and more, with resurgence a chimera.

"But if this is not the German resurgence" — and Herr Hitler thrust out his arms toward his 8,000 listeners and threw out his next words with extraordinary lung power — "if you do not represent the resurgence, there will never be any resurgence for Germany!"

Wild cheers from his hearers followed.

Herr Hitler called on the university students not to stick to pale theory and the seclusion of the study, but come out into the thick of the fight, stand in and with the people and the national movement and thus make a place for themselves in the peoples' confidence.

"There is no real German nation today," he concluded. "What there is of Germany, that is you National Socialists!"

German Citizenship Acquired by Hitler

BY THE NEW YORK TIMES | FEB. 26, 1932

BRUNSWICK, GERMANY, FEB. 25 — Adolf Hitler became a German citizen today through his appointment to the post of Attaché at the Berlin Legation of the State of Brunswick.

A decree authorizing his enfranchisement was signed by Dr. Kuechenthal, the Premier of Brunswick, who belongs to Dr. Alfred Hugenberg's Nationalist party, and Dietrich Klagges, the Minister of the Interior, one of Herr Hitler's chief aides.

The Nazi leader's naturalization under political pressure will not be opposed by the government of the Reich, which has no intention of making a martyr of him on the eve of the election despite official disgust over his refusal to acquire citizenship through the regular channels prescribed for other aliens.

Herr Hitler's new position carries the prerogatives of a diplomat representing one of the minor federate States in the capital of the Reich and will not prevent him from remaining as the chieftain of the Socialist party.

It proved the simplest and speediest solution of a problem which had been long an annoyance to his following and had become pressing, although his defenders held that his four years of war service under the German colors had automatically made him a citizen despite his Austrian birth.

With the collapse of the attempt to enfranchise him in Thuringia in 1930 through a sham appointment to the post of a police sergeant, Brunswick was the only State available to the Nazis for smuggling their leader into the folds of the Reich. It is learned, however, that today's ceremony was carried out with the full knowledge and acquiescence of the Federal Government.

Group Formed by Papen, Hitler Is Named Reich Chancellor

BY GUIDO ENDERIS | JAN. 31, 1933

BERLIN, JAN. 30 — Adolf Hitler, leader of the National Socialist party, today was appointed Chancellor of Germany after being twice rejected last year for that office.

Herr Hitler was manoeuvered into heading a coalition government of National Socialists and Nationalists by Lieut. Col. Franz von Papen, former Chancellor. The new Cabinet is a compromise between a Presidential and a Parliamentary government.

The composition of the Cabinet leaves Herr Hitler no scope for gratification of any dictatorial ambition. He accepted the Chancellorship on less sweeping terms than he laid down in his audiences with the President in August and November of last year. He swore obedience to the republican Constitution today after the President had accepted Colonel von Papen's Cabinet slate.

THE NEW CABINET

The new Cabinet is composed as follows:

Chancellor — Adolf Hitler
Vice Chancellor and Reich Commissioner for Prussia — Lieut. Col. Franz von Papen
Foreign Minister — Baron Constantin von Neurath
Interior Minister — Dr. Wilhelm F. Frick
Defense Minister — General Werner von Blomberg
Finance Minister — Count Lutz Schwerin von Krosigk
Economy and Food Minister — Dr. Alfred Hugenberg
Labor Minister — Franz Seldte
Transportation Minister — Baron Paul Eitz von Ruebenach
Aviation Minister — Hermann Wilhelm Goering
Employment Commissioner — Guenther Gereke

Dr. Frick, former Interior Minister of Thuringia, and Herr Goering are Hitler's leading aides. Baron von Neurath, Count Schwerin von Krosigk and Baron von Ruebenach are holdovers from the Cabinet of Lieut. Gen. Kurt von Schleicher, which fell Saturday. Herr Goering also will be Acting Minister of Interior of Prussia. Herr Seldte is a leader of the Stahlhelm (Steel Helmet veterans' society) and stands far to the Right politically.

ULTIMATUM FROM HINDENBURG

President von Hindenburg had no personal contact with Herr Hitler during the negotiations leading to formation of the Cabinet, but informed quarters say the President threatened to precipitate a Presidential crisis unless Herr Hitler and Dr. Hugenberg made peace and got down to business. This ultimatum enabled Colonel von Papen to round up his new Cabinet without further parleys and march it before President von Hindenburg shortly after noon. It was immediately sworn in.

The speed with which it was projected into office is said to have bewildered Herr Hitler even more than its other members and left him cogitating on whether he had been stampeded into taking the Chancellorship on anything but his own terms.

Colonel von Papen kept his plans so secret that most of the afternoon papers, including Herr Hitler's official organ, were compelled to make over their regular evening editions to tell of the formation of the new Cabinet.

The National Socialists are in a minority in the Cabinet. The Chancellor's Activities are severely limited through the presence in his Cabinet of Colonel von Papen, Baron von Neurath, Count Schwerin von Krosigk, Dr. Hugenberg and Herr Seldte. The preponderance of Conservatives is believed to have decided President von Hindenburg to accept the Nazi chief as Chancellor after his former rejections of him.

The only key post held by the National Socialists is the Interior Ministry, which has jurisdiction over the police. General von Blomberg,

Defense Minister, is an army officer who has not been involved in politics. This portfolio was coveted by the Nazis.

MONEY EXPERIMENTS BARRED

Dr. Hugenberg, Nationalist leader, has financial and economic aims opposed to those of the National Socialists and others in the Cabinet. But Colonel von Papen announced for the new government that "It will not indulge in any economic or currency experimentation."

Some Liberals welcome the new Cabinet. They reason that Herr Hitler has been removed from the street and saddled with the responsibility of office in a setting which will severely circumscribe his liberty of action.

The government will go before the Reichstag Feb. 7. It can survive only with Centrist votes because it has the backing of only 197 National Socialists and 51 Nationalists.

While the Centrist leaders say they were not consulted by Colonel Papen during his scouting expedition in the past two days, it is believed they will be neutral because of the expectation that the Hitler-Papen regime will collapse soon through withdrawal of the National Socialists. It is predicted the Nazis will discover the anomaly of their position in a government in which they hold a minority position with conflicting political groups.

The Socialists are confident Herr Hitler soon will "blow up and be disposed of definitely." But they and the Communists are prepared for repressive measures with Dr. Frick occupying the Interior Ministry. They count on the Reichstag being dissolved if Chancellor Hitler meets a no-confidence vote next week.

NEWSPAPERS SHOW ANXIETY

Newspaper comment, except among National Socialists, reflects general anxiety. "A leap in the dark" is a frequently recurring characterization of the new government.

The Frankfurter Zeitung emphasizes the necessity of rallying "to the defense of the rights of the working population, the fundamentals of democracy, freedom of thought and justice and social and economic rationality."

The Berliner Tageblatt forecasts reaction vieing with Fascism for power. The Democratic party's official bulletin is less alarmed. It says:

> There is the Socialist Hitler under the business supervision of the foxy capitalist Hugenberg and an ex-corporal amidst a Count and four Barons. This Cabinet is better than Papen's because it has some sense at least, namely the disenchantment that will now come to Hitler's followers.

The Nazi utterances naturally are full of elation. "The triumph of tenacity!" exclaims Der Angriff. It continues:

> This is not a mere change in government but is an event like nothing that has preceded in Germany's post-war evolution. With a strong National Socialist advance guard our leaders have moved into the government to clear the road to freedom for the German people.

The Centrist newspaper Germania emphasizes that the Cabinet attempts to unite "the most thoroughgoing capitalism, embodied in Hugenberg, landholding feudalism and Hitler's Socialism." Germania sees benefits because the new Cabinet "has established clearness and unequivocal responsibility in the political situation."

The Koelnische Zeitung hopes Chancellor Hitler will obtain the Centre's toleration "so a Cabinet of national concentration may bring Germany the tranquillity she so urgently needs."

Dr. Hugenberg and the extreme reactionary press are rather restrained considering the circumstances. The Boersen Zeitung admonishes the national front to stand together this time. Dr. Hugenberg's Der Tag deprecates excessive jubilation.

Rule Till 1937 Sought

BY GUIDO ENDERIS | MARCH 21, 1933

IT WAS ANNOUNCED tonight, on the eve of the convocation of the new Reichstag, that the Hitler government would ask it for dictatorial powers lasting until April 1, 1937, or until the replacement of the present Legislature by another.

By the terms of the draft of an empowering act sent to the Reichstag tonight, that body is to be excluded from legislation entirely unless the Cabinet invites its cooperation and the government is to have the right to promulgate laws and decrees outside the channels prescribed by the Constitution, even if they conflict with its provisions.

As the government holds a majority, the passage of the bill is assured, and the Reichstag is expected to adjourn before the end of the week, the measure enabling the Cabinet to carry on without it for at least six months.

The bill contains five articles. The first empowers the government to make laws, including budget laws and loan-authorization laws, and the second says that these loans may deviate from the Constitution in so far as they do not affect the Reichstag and Reichsrat. The rights of the President remain unchanged.

HITLER TO DRAW UP LAWS

The third article provides that the laws made by the government shall be drawn up by the Chancellor, be promulgated in the Legal Gazette and take effect the following day.

Articles LXVIH to LXXVH of the Constitution are not to apply to these laws. These articles comprise the whole section of the Constitution specifying the manner of legislation, including the Reichsrat's power of caveat, the procedure for submitting bills to a national plebiscite, the requiring of a two-thirds majority of two-thirds of the Reichstag's membership for constitutional amendments, the President's duty of proclamation and his power of calling for a plebiscite, etc.

This article would exclude the Reichstag from legislative work entirely unless their cooperation were Invited by the government, and also stipulates that Chancellor Hitler's signature shall suffice in future for the laws of the Reich, which have hitherto been signed by the President.

The fourth article declares that treaties with foreign States relating to objects of Federal legislation shall not require the consent of the legislative bodies for the period of the bill's validity, while the fifth provides that the bill is to take effect with its promulgation and lapse April 1, 1937, or before that, if the present Reichstag is replaced by another.

The Reichstag will be convoked at noon tomorrow in the old Church of the Garrison in Potsdam, where Frederick the Great is buried, and President von Hindenburg will attend the ceremony.

At 5 o'clock in the afternoon the Deputies will meet in the Kroll Opera House in Berlin to organize, as the chamber in the Reichstag Building has not yet been restored following the fire that gutted it a month ago.

GOVERNMENT HAS 52% BACKING

This Reichstag is one chosen by popular suffrage, but under profoundly altered conditions from any obtaining in the numerous parliamentary elections in Germany since the World War. Its dominant National Socialist-Nationalist majority will speak for 52 percent of the electorate, and this 52 percent represents the "national rising."

At least 12,000,000 voters will not be represented in tomorrow's ceremonies in Potsdam, since the Communist Deputies have been proscribed and the Socialists will not attend.

President von Hindenburg acclaimed the day with the following proclamation:

On the day of the solemn opening of the German Reichstag, which, like none of its predecessors since the end of the great war, symbolizes a national State strong in defense, I think in reverence and gratitude of those who fell for Germany.

In steadfast loyalty I greet the dear dead left behind, and in hearty comradeship all my comrades of the great war.

The sacrifices in life and health which that war demanded from Germany have not been in vain. From collapse, Germany is struggling upward again to national strength in the spirit of those who fought and fell for people and Fatherland. A strong German Reich shall be their proud and lasting monument!

A MILITARY SPECTACLE

The ceremonies in Potsdam will present a military spectacle on a scale such as the old Hohenzollern citadel has not witnessed since 1914. The festivities will be initiated by outdoor band concerts at 6:30 A. M. At noon President von Hindenburg and Chancellor Hitler will greet the

Adolf Hitler and President Paul von Hindenburg sit together at a government ceremony with Nazi soldiers in 1933.

new Reichstag in the garrison church, but the service there will be brief because of the adjournment to Berlin for the organizing session.

The celebration will be concluded with a "command" performance of "Die Meistersinger" at the State Opera.

The organizing session, which will witness the election of a presiding staff, should be short since the government bloc will have things pretty much its own way. The reelection of Captain Hermann Wilhelm Goering as President is assured.

The three Vice Presidencies will be allocated to the National Socialists, the Nationalists and the Centrists. The Socialists, although they are the second strongest party in the new Reichstag, will not obtain a position on its staff.

Tomorrow is to be a national holiday throughout the Reich. Dr. Paul Joseph Goebbels, the chief of the new Ministry for National Propaganda and Popular Enlightenment, has ordered all business in Berlin to close from 10 A. M. to 2 P. M. to enable employees and workers to enjoy the program with the aid of loud-speakers that will be posted all over the city. He has arranged a nation-wide hook-up with Potsdam and Berlin and the day's doings will be broadcast to the Reich's humblest hamlet.

Dr. Goebbels is highly impatient with editors who failed to give the official program of tomorrow's festivities the publicity that he had requested. In a rescript to the press tonight he upbraided the offenders for their failure to accommodate the government and requested that they make amends by giving the program renewed publicity in tomorrow's early editions.

"If the press is so little inclined to accede to the government's wishes in this matter, it need not be surprised if the government turns a deaf ear to its wishes and requests in the future," Dr. Goebbels declared.

At about the same hour Berlin's Chief of Police requested the press to announce in bold-face type that the Platz der Republik, the square adjoining the Reichstag building, had officially been re-designated with its old appellation, the Koenigsplatz.

President Backs Hitler

BY OTTO D. TOLISCHUS | JULY 3, 1934

From June 30 to July 2, 1934, a series of extrajudicial killings removed many perceived threats from power, including several prominent members of the Nazi Party. This purge is now known as the Night of the Long Knives.

BERLIN, JULY 2 — The last possible complication in the triumph of Adolf Hitler over the "second revolution" of the Storm Troops was removed today when President von Hindenburg publicly acclaimed his Chancellor's victory.

The aged President, seeking to sustain his failing health at his Summer home at Neudeck, in East Prussia, was informed of events by the press chief of the Propaganda Ministry. Thereupon he sent telegrams that were splashed today across the front pages of the newspapers to show that Germany's revered President and personification of the people's conscience backed Herr Hitler with all the authority that attaches itself in Germany to the name von Hindenburg.

One message, addressed to the Chancellor, said that by crushing "traitorous machinations," Herr Hitler had "rescued the German people from a great danger." A second telegram thanked Prussian Premier Hermann Wilhelm Goering for his "energetic and successful action" in suppressing the attempt at high treason.

The messages were designed especially to counteract rumors circulated today that the killing of alleged conspirators might even lead to the President's resignation.

TOLL MAY BE IN HUNDREDS

Officially, the number of these executions is put at 14 and the total death list at 18. But, according to persistent rumors officially designated as "inaccurate," the total of executions may run into several score and the total death toll into several hundred.

That these deaths threw the President into a grave conflict of conscience cannot be doubted. But the consideration that at the present moment he must choose between supporting Herr Hitler or precipitating chaos by resigning made only one decision possible for the man who chose duty as the guiding principle of his life.

The President's covering authority was needed especially to restore the sinking morale of the official world, which was demoralized by the events of the bloody weekend.

With the Nazi revolution embarked on the course of the French Revolution and with one acting Reich Minister and a former Chancellor already among the dead, a question was raised to official minds as to where the slaughter would end and who might be the next to face the firing squad.

This natural anxiety has not been relieved much by the warning proclamation issued by Dr. Wilhelm Frick, Minister of the Interior, to all officials demanding obedience.

WARNING BY FRICK

Dr. Frick addressed the civil officials of the Reich as follows:

The events of June 30 have shown that there has been an attempt made to pursue an independent policy against the wishes of the Fuehrer [Leader], with the object of creating difficulties for both the Fuehrer and the government and destroying the whole National Socialist State. But the National Socialist State is built up on unconditional obedience to the orders of the Fuehrer and his deputies. The executors of the Fuehrer's will are members of the government and those who take their orders from it, consequently all State officials.

All officials owe unconditional obedience exclusively to their superiors, loyalty and devotion to their official duties. They are responsible to their superiors alone. Although to my knowledge there have been no acts of sabotage in the ranks of the officials, who are accustomed to fulfilling their duty, obeying and observing official regulations, I wish to leave no doubt that I will punish suitably every attempt at disobedience or sabotage of the great work of our Fuehrer.

Every superior has to insure that the officials below him continue uncompromisingly to carry out their duties in every way. Any exceptions are to be reported to me through official channels.

An official statement issued at 2 o'clock this morning had announced that the "purging action" was concluded Sunday night. But up to nearly 3:30 this morning residents of Lichterfelde, a suburb of Berlin, reported hearing the volleys of firing squads in the old military cadet school in their town in which is now located Prussian Premier Goering's police "for special purposes."

The number of executions is still an official secret, which is being revealed very gradually. To the names previously published were added six more today. Five of the dead were Berlin Storm Troop officers. The sixth was Gregor Strasser, former close collaborator of Herr Hitler, who seceded from the party to go with General Kurt von Schleicher during the latter's Chancellorship and who was accused of having conspired with the slain General again.

The Storm Troop officers executed were Divisional Commander Gerth, officer of the Pour le Merite; District Commander Hoffman of the Berlin district; Commander Engels, Berlin district; Commander Konze, Berlin district; and Chief of Staff Sander, Berlin district.

That this list is incomplete is tacitly admitted by the promise that a complete list will be issued tomorrow. Fulfillment of this promise, however, has been repeatedly postponed. The ending of the purging action may, therefore, not have ended the work of the firing squads.

Late tonight, taking cognizance at last of the horrors produced by the summary executions, the press and inspired statements denounce the "nonsensical reports regarding executions in Germany and the fantastic death figures in the émigré press." But the statements disdain to give any figures, adding little to the enlightenment of the world, except in two respects.

It is said that the following persons have not been executed: Bishop Beres of Berlin, General Werner von Fritsch, commander of the army and "other persons named, be they Hohenzollern Princes, Ministers or well-known leaders of the Nazi party."

The statement also objects because "the émigré press suddenly expresses warm sympathy for executed traitors" whom it attacked during their lives as the Nazi press now does at their deaths and it likewise objects to the sympathy of the Marxist émigré press for the Hohenzollern Princes.

Tomorrow the Cabinet is supposed to meet to consider a drastic emergency law to give legal status to the trial of hundreds of prisoners now awaiting an uncertain fate.

Two of these prisoners were officially reported to have been released today. One was Vice Chancellor Franz von Papen. He was said to be at his home, which was found occupied by Schutz Staffel [Special Guard] men. They made it plain that if he was free certainly nobody was free to see him.

The other was Prince August Wilhelm, close friend of Karl Ernst, the executed Storm Troop commander of Berlin. He was called before General Goering, who gave him a good talking to, telling him he had been careless and warning him to drop his "fantastic notions."

The Prince, it is said, replied that he realized the situation, whereupon he was permitted to return home again. A telephone call to his Potsdam home was answered by a voice that sounded like his own. He complained of frequent inquiries regarding his status, but did not clarify it any further.

Hitler Endorsed by 9 to 1 in Poll on His Dictatorship, But Opposition Is Doubled

BY FREDERICK T. BIRCHALL | AUG. 20, 1934

Following Paul von Hindenburg's death on Aug. 2, 1934, the position of president was abolished, further consolidating Hitler's powers under the new title of "Fuehrer," or leader.

BERLIN, MONDAY, AUG. 20 — Eighty-nine and nine-tenths percent of the German voters endorsed in yesterday's plebiscite Chancellor Hitler's assumption of greater power than has ever been possessed by any other ruler in modern times. Nearly 10 percent indicated their disapproval. The result was expected.

The German people were asked to vote whether they approved the consolidation of the offices of President and Chancellor in a single Leader-Chancellor personified by Adolf Hitler. By every appeal known to skillful politicians and with every argument to the contrary suppressed, they were asked to make their approval unanimous.

Nevertheless 10 percent of the voters have admittedly braved possible consequences by answering "No" and nearly 1,000,000 made their answers ineffective by spoiling the simplest of ballots. There was a plain short question and two circles, one labeled "Yes" and the other "No," in one of which the voter had to make a cross. Yet there were nearly 1,000,000 spoiled ballots.

38,279,514 VOTE "YES"

The results given out by the Propaganda Ministry early this morning show that out of a total vote of 43,438,378, cast by a possible voting population of more than 45,000,000, there were 38,279,514 who answered "Yes," 4,287,808 who answered "No" and there were 871,056 defective ballots. Thus there is an affirmative vote of almost 90 percent of the valid votes and a negative vote of nearly 10 percent exclusive of the spoiled ballots which may or may not have been deliberately rendered defective.

How Chancellor Hitler's vote declined is shown by a comparison with the result of the Nov. 12 plebiscite on leaving the Disarmament Conference and the League of Nations. The tabulation follows:

	Yesterday.	**Nov. 12.**
Yes … … … … … … … … … … …	38,279,514	40,600,243
No … … … … … … … … … … …	4,287,808	2,101,004
Invalid … … … … … … … … … ..	871,056	750,282
Percent of no's … … … … … … …	9.8	4.8

Members of the Nazi party ride through Berlin on Aug. 19, 1934, waving the Nazi flag and a banner encouraging Germans to vote "Yes" on the plebiscite supporting Hitler's assumption of the responsibility of the presidency.

These results therefore show that the number of Germans discontented with Chancellor Hitler's course is increasing but is not yet seriously damaging to it. He is the Fuehrer of the Reich with absolute power by the vote of almost 90 percent of the Germans in it but the number of dissentients has doubled since the last test.

It is not yet a matter for international concern but there are other considerations which may he.

DICTATORSHIP NOW COMPLETE

The endorsement gives Chancellor Hitler, who four years ago was not even a German citizen, dictatorial powers unequaled in any other country, and probably unequaled in history since the days of Genghis Khan. He has more power than Joseph Stalin in Russia, who has a party machine to reckon with; more power than Premier Mussolini of Italy who shares his prerogative with the titular ruler; more power than any American President ever dreamed of.

No other ruler has so widespread powers nor so obedient and compliant subordinates. The question that interests the outside world now is what Chancellor Hitler will do with such unprecedented authority.

Nazi opinion is not disposed to be altogether cheerful about the result. When one high official was asked by this correspondent to comment on it he said:

"Obviously we feel the effects of June 30."

He referred to the execution of Ernst Roehm and other Storm Troop chiefs.

That is also the opinion of many other Germans, especially among the more substantial classes. They interpret the result as the beginning of a protest against the rule of arbitrary will and as an effort to force Chancellor Hitler back to the rule of law.

In their view the vote may induce the Fuehrer to steer henceforth a more moderate course and take account of the sensibilities of general opinion. Some of the more optimistic even hope it may induce him to get rid of some of his radical advisers, to whom the opposition within Germany is great.

This view, however, is not shared generally and the dissent is borne out by the remark of a Nazi official who said bitterly, "We have become too soft."

EX-MARXISTS SUPPORT HITLER

A feature of the election was that former Marxists cast a far heavier vote for Chancellor Hitler than the so-called bourgeoisie. In Berlin especially, judging by their vote, former Communists still are Leader Hitler's most loyal followers. In one voting district in Wedding, where a few years ago Communists fought from behind barricades against the police, the "yes" votes amounted to 949; the "no" votes and invalid ballots totaled 237.

In one district west of Berlin, inhabited mainly by business men and intellectuals, the "yes" vote was only 840 and the "no" votes and invalid ballots totaled 351. Other tests provided similar results.

In the Communist districts protest votes with Communist inscriptions were rare. In Western Berlin they were more frequent. In one district five ballots had the name "Thaelmann" written in. (Ernst Thaelmann is an imprisoned Communist leader.)

One ballot contained this inscription, "Since nothing has happened to me so far I vote 'Yes.' " It was signed "Non-Aryan."

Interesting also are the following results: The hospital of the Jewish community in one district cast 168 "Yes" votes, 92 "Noes," and 46 ballots were invalid. The Jewish Home for Aged People in another district cast 94 "Yes" votes, four "Noes" and three invalid ballots. This vote is explainable, of course, by the fear of reprisals if the results from these Jewish institutions had been otherwise. It is paralleled by other results outside Berlin.

In all Bavaria Chancellor Hitler received the largest vote in his favor in the concentration camp at Dachau where 1,554 persons voted "Yes" and only eight "No" and there were only ten spoiled ballots.

HAMBURG LEADS OPPOSITION

Hamburg, which only two days ago gave Herr Hitler the most enthusiastic reception he had ever received anywhere, led the country in the opposition vote. The official figures were: Total vote cast. 840,000; "Yes." 651,000; "No," 168,000; invalidated ballots, 21,000.

The "No" vote, in other words, was 20 percent of the total vote. Counting the invalid ballots as negative in intent, the total opposition votes exceeded 22 percent. The percentage of the electorate voting was 92.4.

Hamburg is the home city of Ernst Thaelmann and on his triumphant entry into the city on Friday Herr Hitler made it a point to drive past Herr Thaelmann's former home.

As far as observers could ascertain, the election everywhere was conducted with perfect propriety, and secrecy of the ballot was safeguarded. The ballots were marked in regular election booths and placed in envelopes and these were put in the ballot boxes. After the voting had ended the ballot box was emptied on a large table and the vote was counted publicly in the regular manner. Appraising of individual votes seemed impossible.

One check on possible non-voters, however, was exercised by instructions that the voting authorizations issued to those who for one reason or another planned to be outside their regular voting district on election day must be returned unless used. The number of such authorizations issued for this election exceeded anything known before.

Throughout the day Storm Troopers stood before each polling place with banners calling on the voters to vote "Yes." Otherwise voters remained unmolested. Inside the polling places uniforms and even party emblems had been forbidden, but the execution of this order was lax. In some apparently doubtful districts brown uniforms dominated the scene as a warning to would-be opponents.

NAZIS TRY FOR RECORD VOTE

All past efforts in getting out the German vote were eclipsed in this election. During Saturday night a huge final poster was plastered on billboards everywhere. It said:

> Your leader [Hitler] has traveled 1,500,000 kilometers by airplane, railway and motor car in the cause of Germany's rebirth. You have but to walk 100 meters to your voting booth to vote "yes."

All over Germany means were taken to get the Sunday late-sleeping population out of bed early. The polls opened at 8 o'clock, but in Berlin Storm Troops, Hitler Youth Troops and Nazi labor union groups took to the streets as early as 6 o'clock to wake the populace by shouting at them to do their duty. Many of these groups had bugles or drum corps and an occasional band was heard.

In Munich 25 brass bands started marching through the city about the same hour with the same object. At Frankfurt-am-Main Storm Troops' bands played at the most important street intersections all morning.

At Erfurt late Saturday night Storm Troopers with torches marched the streets, and soon after daybreak again were under way shouting to the citizens to get up and vote. In Bremen all the church hells rang for 15 minutes before 8 o'clock. In Karlsruhe saluting cannon reinforced the brass bands.

BERLIN GOES TO POLLS EARLY

The result was that at Berlin's 27 polling places throughout the morning there were long lines before each, waiting to vote. In the working class districts crowds assembled before the polling places were opened. By 11 o'clock 40 percent of the vote had been polled, but all day trucks equipped with buglers and cheering corps went through the city rallying the laggards.

Ambulances for the sick voters and volunteered private cars for the aged and infirm were busy all day. The polls were open until 6 o'clock, but in the late afternoon comparatively few votes were registered. The voting had been done.

An odd feature of the election was the large number of voters who voted outside their home districts. This is the holiday season, so 2,500,000 had special permission to vote away from home. Four Saxon cities granted 130,000 such permissions to vote in other parts of the Reich.

At the central railway station in Munich 10,000 travelers had voted in 13 special booths set up there before 11 o'clock. Polling places were set up along the wall of the Kiel Canal for sailors on German ships.

In foreign ports German Consuls hired vessels and took voters out to the high seas, making a celebration of it. Lieut. Col. Franz von Papen, envoy to Vienna, came back to Berlin from Austria to vote.

In Berlin enthusiasm was skillfully maintained by every conceivable device. Around the chancellery, where Chancellor Hitler slept, there was a crowd from daybreak onward. By 8 o'clock the police had to rope off Wilhelmstrasse for through traffic.

A loud-speaker in an open window in the Propaganda Ministry across the street led the crowd In singing Nazi songs. During the day Chancellor Hitler appeared in a chancellery window about 12 times and was madly cheered.

At all important traffic centres in Cologne busts of Chancellor Hitler had been set up and at the polling places his picture was wreathed in evergreens hung over the entrances. All cities were beflagged as for a triumph.

In Breslau the polling places were decked with flowers and there were long parades of Storm Troopers and war veterans through the streets all day. At Neudeck the 96 voters of the Hindenburg manor went to the polls in a body to vote "yes."

More to attain the universal "joyous affirmation" that all Nazi speakers demanded throughout the campaign could hardly have been done.

Reich Adopts Swastika as Nation's Official Flag, Anti-Jewish Laws Passed

BY OTTO D. TOLISCHUS | SEPT. 16, 1935

NUREMBERG, GERMANY, SEPT. 15 — National Socialist Germany definitely flung down the gauntlet before the feet of Western liberal opinion tonight when the Reichstag, assembled for a special session here in connection with the "Party Day of Freedom," decreed a series of laws that put Jews beyond the legal and social pale of the German nation, and in token of this act proclaimed the swastika banner to be the sole flag of the German Reich.

With this action, in the words of Reichstag President Goering, begins the next step of "National Socialist upbuilding," generally being called here the second revolution, the first part having been concluded with Germany's rearmament, in honor of which the present party conclave bears its name.

PROVISIONS OF NEW LAWS

The new laws provide:

1. German citizenship with full political rights depends on the special grant of a Reich citizenship charter, to be given only to those of German or racially related blood, who have proved by their attitude that they are willing and fit loyally to serve the German people and the Reich.

This deprives Jews of German citizenship but leaves them the status of "State members" (Staatsangehoeriger), and Germans found undeserving of Reich citizenship may likewise be reduced to this status, which, among other disadvantages, entails loss of the vote.

2. Marriages between Jews and citizens of German or racially related blood, as well as extra-marital sexual relations between them, are forbidden and will be punished by penal servitude or imprisonment. Jews must not engage feminine domestic help of German or racially related

blood under 45 years old. Jews likewise are forbidden to show the Ger-
man national flag, but may under protection of the State show the Jewish
colors of white and blue. Violations of the last two provisions are punish-
able by imprisonment up to one year or a fine or both.

3. The Reich, or national, flag is the swastika flag, which is also the flag
of commerce to be flown by German merchant ships. But a special war
flag is to be fixed by Hitler and the War Minister, which is expected to
follow the present black, white and red flag and will probably contain the
swastika cross in place of the iron cross for a symbol.

REICHSTAG IS VOICELESS

Those laws, which General Goering himself called momentous, were introduced with speeches by Hitler and General Goering and adopted unanimously and with many cheers by the Reichstag, which by like unanimity and cheers rendered itself voiceless at the beginning of the session.

At the request of Dr. Wilhelm Frick, Minister of the Interior, the Reichstag abolished its own rules of procedure and placed itself "under the principle of leadership," to be exercised by General Goering. This motion is as important as any of the laws passed, for it formally abolished the Reichstag as a deliberative body and reduced it to a mere division of the National Socialist party. That, Dr. Frick explained, brought the Reichstag in step with the new epoch.

Hitler's speech, revised at the last minute, was remarkably short and was delivered in a rather weakened voice. But the Fuehrer had been under tremendous physical strain during the last few days and today. He delivered one speech this morning and for five hours stood in the Nuremberg market place reviewing the march of 120,000 men of various National Socialist formations, which demonstrated the physical force behind the laws passed tonight.

In his Reichstag speech Hitler motivated the laws themselves by again putting into the foreground his assertion in the early part of the Nazi conclave that Jews were propagators of bolshevism and in this connection he referred to the Bremen flag incident and the verdict of Magistrate Brodsky, saying:

> *The insult to the German flag — which has been settled in the most loyal manner by the American Government — is an illustration of the attitude of Jewry toward Germany, even when it is in an official capacity, and an effective confirmation of the rightness of our National Socialist legislation, the aim of which is to prevent similar incidents in our administration and jurisprudence.*

For the rest, however, he merely mentioned the alleged "provocative" efforts and new anti-German boycott agitation on the part of the Jews, and he made a specific reference to alleged Jewish demonstrations against the anti-Jewish one in Berlin, which were given at the time as a reason for the Kurfuerstendamm riots that initiated the present anti-Jewish drive, now realized.

ASSAILS MEMEL "OPPRESSION"

Most of the speech was devoted to foreign policy, in which connection, in pronounced contrast with the National Socialist treatment of Jews, he sharply protested against the "mistreatment and oppression" of Germans in the Memel territory. He demanded that Lithuania be held, "before Mussolini," to observe treaties, and suggested such action by the League as Germany had met before the problem "assumes a form that some day may be regretted by all powers."

Similarly, a strong tone was taken against Moscow and the Communist International, but at the same time Hitler also renewed his repeated protestations of "unshakable love for peace" and proclaimed Germany's neutrality in "things which do not affect her."

"The purport of the new army, which is to demonstrate its might tomorrow," he said, was not to threaten the freedom of any European nation, nor to consume the reserves of National Socialism's reconstruction work in "frivolous and insane adventures" but finally to safeguard the freedom of the German people.

GIVES WARNING TO JEWS

In proposing the explicit laws against Jews, Hitler said the German Government was trying to avert incalculable defensive action by an indignant population, and guided by that fact "through a single secular solution a level will, perhaps, he created enabling the German people to find tolerable relations with Jewish people." But he added:

> If this hope should not be realized and if international Jewish agitation should continue, the situation will have to be reconsidered.

"If the attempt at legal regulation fails again," the Fuehrer added, "the problem will have to he transferred from law to the National Socialist party for a final solution."

This avoidance for the present of the threatened enabling act, which would have legally delivered the Jews to the mercy of individual party members, as well as the enactment of any special economic restrictions, aside from the professional restrictions imposed, was regarded here tonight as a victory, such as it is, for Dr. Hjalmar Schacht, Minister of Economics.

On the other hand, the implications of the laws and the actual status of Jews in Germany are still wholly unclear and will depend entirely on administrative enforcement of regulations still to be issued by Dr. Frick and Rudolf Hess, Minister without portfolio. If the law puts Jews in a status similar to that of aliens they may be subjected to further economic restrictions as well.

In his final declaration to the Reichstag, Hitler told the Deputies they had passed laws "whose effect would be recognized only after many centuries," and he appealed to them to take care that the nation did not leave the way of law and asserted that these laws "are enabled by unprecedented discipline of the whole German people, for which you are responsible."

For some it appeared symbolic that after a beautiful day a steady downpour of rain started just as the Reichstag let out, and it was also a fitting touch that as Hitler returned to his hotel with a drawn and unsmiling face, in spite of cheering crowds, he was greeted at the entrance by Julius Streicher, anti-Semitic leader, who on his countenance registered his victory.

In accordance with the new "parliamentary leadership principle" General Goering extended the debate by giving a lengthy speech from the President's seat. The new flag law, he said, was necessary. He ridiculed those who seek compromise with national socialism by hiding behind the old imperial emblem, and he likewise attacked Jews as "race destroyers" and asserted "German women and girls must be protected." There were no other remarks.

The Reichstag was the first called in Nuremberg in 400 years. It met in an improvised hall in the house of the Cultural Association and was attended by the entire Cabinet, with Foreign Minister von Neurath and especially General Werner von Blomberg, Defense Minister, Dr. Frick and General Walter von Reichenau, head of the War Academy, prominent among the government representatives.

Hitler Glorified at Nazi Art Show

BY THE NEW YORK TIMES | JULY 17, 1937

MUNICH, GERMANY, JULY 16 — The "Festival of German Art" that is to precede the dedication of a new art gallery here Sunday by Chancellor Adolf Hitler opened today with much speech-making in this city, which by the Fuehrer's decree has received the honorary title of "City of German Art."

Elaborate is a mild word to describe the official preview of this exhibition of the art that has blossomed forth since National Socialism came into power. Photographs published in the local newspapers show that examples of the old "Jugend" style of painting of the early part of this century hang side by side with Nazi examples of painting and sculpture.

Adolf Wagner, Bavarian Minister of the Interior, opened the show with a speech in which he hailed Hitler as "the greatest builder of all time" and "not only the patron of German art but its greatest master."

After eulogizing Hitler as the creator of a new German unity, which, he added, had rescued the German people from decline and destruction and "made it an immortal nation," Mr. Wagner continued:

> But transcending all else in greatness and security as witnessed in this exhibition is the certainty that today and in all other ages there does not and did not exist a civilization without Deutsche Kultur. What a glorious privilege it is to belong to a people of which this can be said without presumption!

The occasion was one on which National Socialist political achievements were praised as well as German art under Nazi rule. Mr. Wagner characterized the event as "the rebirth of German art," and in another speech before newspaper men declared among other things that "Adolf Hitler is the greatest of living German artists."

In the future, Mr. Wagner predicted, German artists would no longer have to go abroad for study. To go to Munich and contemplate the art treasures there would be "sufficient."

Another feature of the festival is gala performances of German opera, classical dramas, open-air concerts and ballets. Sunday there will be a street procession forming a pageant of 2,000 years of German culture. There will also be dancing in the squares, in which the public is invited to take part.

Hitler Hails Ties with Italy, Japan

BY THE NEW YORK TIMES | SEPT. 8, 1937

NUREMBERG, GERMANY, SEPT. 7 — Chancellor Adolf Hitler warned the world as the National Socialist party congress opened this morning that it would "no longer be possible to disregard at any time and place" the "community of will" between Nazi Germany and Fascist Italy.

He also asserted that the Reich's treaty with Japan "serves the same purpose of unity in repelling an attack on the civilized world that today may come in Spain, tomorrow in the East and the day afterward somewhere else."

The Fuehrer's declarations were contained in the annual party proclamation, drafted by him but read to the first assembly of the congress by Adolf Wagner, Bavarian Nazi leader.

THREE POINTS ARE STRESSED

In the proclamation's sole but highly significant reference to German foreign policy of the future, Hitler said:

> I should like to make three points: first, the Treaty of Versailles is dead [applause]; second, Germany is free [more applause]; third, the guarantee of our liberty is our army [tremendous applause].
>
> If National Socialism had no more to say for itself than these three results of its leadership and energy, by these alone it would be entitled to a place of honor in our nation's annals.
>
> Our army is barely four years old, but on the other hand Germany is no longer isolated but is united in close friendship with powerful States.
>
> The community of interests between National Socialist Germany and Fascist Italy has revealed itself in the last few months to be more and more an element for safeguarding Europe from chaotic madness. In the future it will no longer be possible to disregard at any time and place this community of will.

Benito Mussolini (left) and Adolf Hitler (right) ride together at a parade in Munich, Germany, during one of Mussolini's visits to Germany.

Our treaty with Japan serves the same purpose of unity in repelling an attack on the civilized world that today may come in Spain, tomorrow in the East and the day afterward somewhere else.

We are filled with strong hope that other powers may understand the symptoms of the times in order to reinforce this front of reason for the protection of our peace and culture.

Nazis Pay Tribute: Millions in Berlin Hail Hitler as Leader on His 50th Birthday

BY OTTO. D. TOLISCHUS | APRIL 21, 1939

BERLIN, APRIL 20 — The flower of Germany's armed forces, represented by some 40,000 troops from all arms and services and showing all the guns and mechanical equipment they possess, paraded for four hours today before Chancellor Hitler and his paladins, before the diplomatic corps and some 2,000,000 cheering persons along the new five-mile fantastically decorated Via Triumphalis — the German Champs Elysees — in what the press hails as the "greatest parade on earth."

This military spectacle, surpassing everything staged hitherto even in the Reich and impressive both for its businesslike grimness and its discipline, marked the climax of the celebration of Herr Hitler's fiftieth birthday, which is being observed with such lavish pomp that it is already popularly called the "10-million-mark birthday party."

For four hours, from 11:25 A. M. to 3:25 P. M., the Via Triumphalis resounded to the tramp of marching men, the clatter of horses' hoofs and, most of all, the roar of motorized units, which dominated the parade while 162 planes of all kinds thundered overhead.

HITLER STANDS ON DAIS

Herr Hitler himself, clad in his usual simple brown uniform, stood on a raised dais covered with red plush and furnished with a gilded throne-like chair over which was spread a gray canopy decorated with National Socialist eagles and the iron cross. The weather, however, was so good that the canopy was rolled up most of the time.

Flanking him in separate boxes were the titular rulers of Great Germany's protectorates and dependencies — to the left Baron Constantin von Neurath, Protector for Bohemia-Moravia, in a field gray diplomatic uniform, and State President Emil Hacha, a lone, forlorn-looking civilian in top hat. To the right was Dr. Joseph Tiso and the Slovak delegation.

Behind Herr Hitler in full uniform were Field Marshal Hermann Goering, Colonel-General Walther von Brauchitsch, Commander-in-Chief of the army; Colonel-General Wilhelm Keitel, head of the Supreme Command of the armed forces; Grand Admiral Erich Raeder, Commander in Chief of the navy, and a galaxy of other generals.

On the other side of the street, opposite Herr Hitler's dais, sat the leading men of State and party and the diplomatic corps, among whom were the red-capped Spanish Falangistas led by General José Moscardo, the Alcazar's defender. Bareheaded Mgr. Cesare Orsenigo, the Papal Nuncio, attracted most eyes because it was the first time he had attended a military spectacle.

Stretching along both sides of the road for the whole five miles were 2,000,000 men, women and children, for it was a national holiday with pay and National Socialist organizing ability knows how to turn out masses.

MILITARY ATTACHÉS ATTENTIVE

While the parade was staged in honor of Herr Hitler's birthday, it was also staged for the benefit of the world generally, the smaller European States particularly, as a demonstration of German might and German determination to establish a "German peace" in Europe despite Polish defiance, British "encirclement" and President Roosevelt's "meddling."

And the military attachés who in their many-colored uniforms sat next to Herr Hitler's dais were therefore the most interested and most attentive spectators. Many of them, most particularly the Polish military attaché, accordingly, were seen watching every detail and taking copious notes. Every European government, undoubtedly, had detailed accounts tonight of any military innovations showed.

Paraders march past Adolf Hitler during the celebration of his 50th birthday in Berlin.

But, however resplendent the spectacle may have been, it was something of a disappointment from this specialized viewpoint. There was little new, and even that had been known to exist.

For the German crowds and foreign laymen there was a two-fold sensation — a company of the first parachute regiment, clad in flat steel helmets and green-gray, baggy uniforms, with parachutes strapped on behind, and what the program designated as Germany's heaviest artillery. This latter consisted of four 24-centimeter [about 10-inch] cannon which looked almost like naval guns. Each was transported in four sections on four trucks, each of which, again, was drawn by a tractor, while the gun crew numbered 30 men. Both the parachute men and the heavy artillery drew the biggest applause from the crowd, the latter even more than the former.

But those militarily minded who knew of parachute troops and had seen a sample of heavy guns in previous parades centered their interest on two other displays. One was the entirely new 130-millimeter [about 5-inch] anti-aircraft gun transported in two sections on two trucks drawn by tractors, which is as big as anti-aircraft guns come and probably bigger than most countries possess.

The second was the Skoda 15-centimeter [about 6-inch] cannon also transported in two loads and apparently taken over from the former Czech Army now being disbanded.

Aside from these there was infantry, afoot and motorized, horse and motorized cavalry, horse and motorized artillery of all calibers, air defense troops and anti-aircraft artillery of all calibers, motorcycle and bicycle troops. There were pioneer divisions with pontoons and air defense troops with elaborate searchlights and sound detectors, communications divisions and last but not least more than 100 tanks of all weights and sizes from the well known small German tank with two machine guns to the twenty-ton tank with a 37-millimeter [1.5-inch] gun which is the heaviest the Germans have.

Each tank has received a name. Most of them seem to have been taken from newly acquired places such as Prague, Karlsbad, Memel and the like.

PLANES PRECEDE HITLER'S CAR

The spectacle began with a parade of 162 airplanes, which preceded and followed Herr Hitler's car. As far as is ascertainable no new types were shown and although the show was impressive the line-up of planes appeared somewhat ragged. They were followed by the arrival of bands of the various troops which relieved one another during the parade and behind them came the banner battalion carrying 300 regimental banners from various army units which lined up opposite Herr Hitler's dais.

Most of the parading troops belonged to training divisions that had set the pace for the rest of the army and the regiment "Great Germany," which consists of picked men from all over the Reich and is looked on as the new guard, the old Kaiser's guard having been abolished. They came mainly from Potsdam, Gera, Hamburg and Weimar.

At the same time troops that had been set in march ostensibly for the parade never showed up in it and even the airfleet was held to be comparatively meager, which may or may not have been due to the early cloudy weather, which later cleared. Whether the parade also was used as a cover for troop movements for other purposes of course was not known.

CROWDS CHEER HITLER

Despite the strained international situation the crowds appeared to regard the military spectacle this time with comparative optimism. The enthusiasm perhaps was not quite so boisterous as on previous occasions, but the crowd's mood was also far from the deadly, ominous silence meeting the troops marching through Berlin last December. During the parade sections of the crowd started cheering Herr Hitler.

But the military spectacle soon recaptured their attention and kept these cheers from attaining standard volume. Only two incidents interfered with the otherwise matchless perfection of the parade. The drummer's horse on the mounted artillery band stationed before Herr Hitler started to rear so the drummer had to cease drumming and the tail end of the tank division, which concluded the parade and which was passing by at some 40 miles an hour, got jammed right in front of the Chancellor because of a traffic obstruction.

Foes Are Warned

BY THE NEW YORK TIMES | MAY 2, 1939

BERLIN, MAY 1 — In May Day speeches today Chancellor Adolf Hitler assailed the boycott of German goods in the United States, appealed to labor for national unity and increased production and denounced the "warmongers and panic-makers" of the democracies.

The Chancellor spoke three times in programs that were part of today's mammoth popular festival in Berlin, which was marked by parades throughout the day by 1,500,000 men, women and children and was concluded tonight by Maypole ceremonies in the Lustgarten.

In two of his speeches Herr Hitler put emphasis on the need for internal unity, and this plea was repeated in a talk by Field Marshal Hermann Goering.

Late this afternoon the Chancellor left for Bavaria, where he is to remain a fortnight. Startling developments in international politics apparently are not expected by the Foreign Office, although the press gives considerable space to reports from London alleging that British newspapers are promoting a biased pro-Polish sentiment.

WARNS YOUTH IT MUST FIGHT

Early in the day Herr Hitler motored to the Olympic Stadium, where he addressed 100,000 boys and girls of the Hitler Youth, who awaited him in a colorful formation that spread over the entire arena. The keynote of his brief speech there was an admonition to defend the national colors. He told the boys and girls that they would have to fight for their rights because nothing would come their way as a free gift.

At noon Herr Hitler addressed a huge meeting of workers banked around the 175-foot, gayly beribboned Maypole in the Lustgarten. In this speech he called for national unity, stressed the importance of productivity to the national economy and assailed foreign critics of his regime.

Herr Hitler declared he preferred to depend "on the word of the German people and on the Western fortifications rather than assertions by governments that have become victims of warmongers and panicmakers." Referring to the boycott in the United States, he declared:

I believe it would have been more rational to import German commodities rather than the most inferior German subjects. We can be only happy to get rid of them and are content to leave it to others to get on with them. We shall see to it that they do not threaten us, and I have made every provision in advance for such a contingency.

UNITY HELD VITAL TO EXISTENCE

National unity, the Chancellor asserted, is a vital factor in Germany's "fight for existence."

"Without unity we cannot solve our national problems," he said.

We are sworn to each other for success or failure. If any one ever doubted this, he must recognize it now in the attitude of the rest of the world toward us. Are not the same old encirclement politicians at work again?

I believe it is necessary for all Germans to throw aside their old prejudices and draw together in the common conviction that, united, we can withstand any danger; divided, however, we shall fall.

You will understand why I place no faith in the words of those who are in the service of warmongers and agitators. I depend alone upon you, my German people. All honor to declarations of the League of Nations — to my mind the fortifications on Germany's western border are a better guarantee of our freedom.

The first principle of a nation is that its life depends on its living space. The greater the problem the greater must be the efforts toward its solution. We can solve our problems only if we unitedly pursue these efforts. That is why national unity is a vital necessity.

Individual freedom must be subjected to the nation's interests, Herr Hitler declared, and he proclaimed "the security of Germany's living space as the highest law of the land."

PRODUCTION AT TOP OF PROGRAM

In emphasizing the importance of production, which "has been placed at the head of the National Socialist economic program," the Chancellor asserted:

We have learned to procure most of our vital needs by increased production. We have, however, also the problem of our living space, which is vital to the victory or defeat of a nation.

The foreign press was again a target of Herr Hitler's wrath and ridicule. He denounced the "snowball system of lies," which, he said, grow bigger the more they are denied.

"Sometimes I think these creatures of the press are a special form of brain parasite," the Chancellor declared.

They always know what I am thinking — they knew what I would say in my speech today even before I did.

These warmongers, who never achieved anything themselves, are the ones who want to drive the world into fresh catastrophes. They do not want peace because they do nothing to insure peace. They think they know everything, but they really do not know anything.

The May Day ceremonies began early in the morning with the traditional "youths' greeting" in the Olympic Stadium. Baldur von Schirach, leader of the Hitler Youth, and Propaganda Minister Joseph Goebbels briefly addressed the 100,000 boys and girls assembled there prior to Herr Hitler's arrival.

In his speech the Chancellor said:

The time has passed when youth must feel ashamed of its elders. For centuries the world denied us our vital rights. Those days are gone; they will find their final consummation in you, the youth of Germany, and it is necessary that you realize this responsibility while you are yet young.

There are nations around us that do not desire German unity. This is because they do not want to grant us our vital rights. We have regained these rights, and it may be that we shall have to defend them. In that I rely on you, and when the hour comes, when the world tries to encroach on German freedom, I trust that from millions of throats of Germany's youth will burst a cry that will show the world once and for all that the time of German disintegration is past.

RECEIVES CONTEST WINNERS

This afternoon Herr Hitler received in the new Chancellery 141 winners of the "Efficiency Contests of German Enterprises." In a brief speech he stressed once more the importance of increased production. Later he invited all to be his guests for coffee and cake.

Tonight Marshal Goering concluded the day's speeches with another passionate plea for Germany unity:

So long as the German nation is united we can defy all comers and remain invincible," he said. "Our unity will bring forth all the latent forces that for centuries slumbered in our people. We threaten no one, but we guard our honor just as we guard our security, and we are ready to risk all in its defense.

Threats or attempts at intimidation will be met with our united strength. The Fuehrer reawakened faith in our might, and never again will any power in the world be able to destroy it.

A military tattoo before the Chancellery and a pyrotechnical display brought the day's ceremonies to a close.

CHAPTER 4

Hitler at War

On Sept. 1, 1939, years of broken promises and provocations by Hitler at last erupted in an invasion of Poland, sparking the beginning of World War II. Initially successful in his conquest of Europe, Hitler was praised by a German populace eager for "Lebensraum," or "living room." Journalists — and indeed the world at large — carefully watched the man behind the German war machine, questioning his sanity, trying to predict his coming moves and determining how, if at all, he could be stopped.

Hitler Tells the Reichstag 'Bomb Will Be Met by Bomb'

BY THE NEW YORK TIMES | SEPT. 1, 1939

CHANCELLOR ADOLF HITLER of Germany, in a world broadcast this morning, opened "a fight until the resolution of the situation" against Poland, announcing that "from now on bomb will be met by bomb."

At the same time he announced, to face any eventuality, that if anything "happened" to him, Field Marshal Hermann Goering was to be in charge; if to Marshal Goering, Rudolph Hess; if to Herr Hess, the Senate, which he proposes to appoint, will select a successor.

The Chancellor, after attempting to narrow the conflict with Poland by assuring the Western powers that he had no designs on their frontiers, by assuring the neutrality of the sideline powers and by acknowledging the friendliness of Italy and the new relations with Russia, issued a defy to Poland's allies.

SAYS HE WILL CARRY ON

"I shall carry on this fight regardless of against whom I may come," he declared.

At the same time he held the door open for Poland to capitulate to his demands, declaring that he did not intend to make war against women and children. He said that if a solution did not come from the present Polish Government, it would come from a future Polish Government.

The Chancellor expressed confidence, toward the close of his address, that his decision, which was being broadcast over amplifiers hastily erected by electricians at the last moment in the streets of Berlin and the provincial capitals, would be accepted by the German people.

The scene enacted in the Kroll Opera House in Berlin was carried over sound waves to most of the nations of the world. From Berlin hook-ups had been arranged with the three major networks of the United States, and, according to the announcer for the German broadcasting system, over the Italian, Hungarian, Spanish, Norwegian, Swedish, Danish, Yugoslav, British and French national networks. The summons to the Reichstag, ordered by Herr Hitler himself, had been sent out only a few hours before the meeting. Most of the members had been awaiting the signal, and when the opera house opened shortly before 10 o'clock [5 o'clock, New York time] this morning, they were dressed in the uniforms of their military formations.

After Herr Hitler finished speaking the deputies enacted a law incorporating Danzig into the Reich, declaring Danzig citizens were now Germans, voiding the Constitution of the Free City and extending to its territory the jurisdiction of German law.

At 5:10 A. M., Marshal Goering opened the meeting and turned the floor over to the Chancellor.

In the early part of his address, Herr Hitler electrified his audience with this declaration:

We have all been suffering under the tortures that the Versailles treaty has been inflicting upon us.

Then, speaking with measured deliberateness of Germany's claims to the pre-war German areas, he announced, as he had on a previous occasion:

The Treaty of Versailles is, for us Germans, and has been, for us Germans, not a law.

Anticipating what the announcement's reiteration would lead to, the Deputies roared applause. Then Herr Hitler, his indignation rising as he proceeded, set about building up the German case, asserting that his proposals for a peaceful solution of the problem of Danzig and the Polish Corridor had been rejected, and charging that the Poles had visited atrocities on Germans, especially women and children, "killing many of them."

SUMMARY OF SPEECH

A summary of Herr Hitler's speech was translated as follows:

For months we have been suffering under the burdens of the Treaty of Versailles. Danzig was and is a German city. All these regions have only Germany to thank for their cultural development.

Minorities in the Polish Corridor have been shamefully mistreated. Here, as in other respects, I have tried to solve the problems by peaceful means. In the fifteen years of National Socialism we have been trying to solve problems peacefully.

I have often made proposals for the righting of insufferable wrongs. All of these suggestions which I have made for peaceful solutions, including disarmament, redevelopment and limitation of warfare, have been rejected.

The long list of proposals I have made, including disarmament and limitation of warfare, have been rejected. All have been in vain.

An impossible situation has arisen. The Treaty of Versailles for us Germans is not a law. It is not fair to put a pistol to a man's head, starve him and then say you are acting under sacred law.

As to Danzig and the Corridor, I have tried to effect a peaceful solution.

An impossible situation has arisen. The Treaty of Versailles is not law; therefore we are not violating any law.

HIS PROPOSAL REJECTED

I cannot be indifferent to the fate of Danzig. I have had formulated proposals, and I must say nothing could be more fair than these proposals. My proposals were rejected — by mobilizations and pressure on the German people in the Polish Corridor and in Danzig.

I told the Polish Ambassador ten days ago that if this situation continued, if Danzig was persecuted and if attempts continued by Poland to ruin Danzig economically, the situation could not be tolerated.

It has been maintained that persecutions have not been carried out by the Poles, but I would like to know what are persecutions if not the mistreatment of women and children, in many places where they have even been killed. I made one last effort to make a proposal for mediation to the British Government. I accepted the British proposal.

I accepted the preparations for mediation and I waited for the Polish representative two days.

If Germany should stand for such things, Germany has nothing left but to withdraw from the political stage. No one should confuse my patience for cowardice.

The first answer I received as a reply from Poland was mobilization and the atrocities committed against German women and children.

I have therefore decided to talk to Poland in the same language she has used toward us for such a long time. Not for one second shall I hesitate in fulfillment of my duty.

I have offered England friendship and, if necessary, close cooperation. Germany has no interests in the West. The Westwall is and remains our border in the west.

Members of the Reichstag salute Adolf Hitler in Berlin's Kroll Opera House following his speech justifying the invasion of Poland, which initiated World War II.

I should like to express at this time our thanks to Italy.

Neutral powers have assured us of their neutrality and we have assured them they will be respected. We mean this.

HAILS PACT WITH RUSSIA

I am happy to make an announcement. I see no reason why Russia and Germany should remain enemies any longer. Any war between our peoples would be of no profit to either. We have, therefore, decided that the use of force would give an advantage to others. We have resolved to draw up a pact to exclude the use of force for all time to come.

Every attempt of the western powers to change the situation will fail. This pact means — for all time in the future — something definite and something we will stick to and hold by. I believe the whole German nation will greet this stand.

Germany and Russia fought against each other in the World War, and that shall not occur again. The ratification of the German-Russian [non-aggression] pact was announced yesterday in Berlin. I can endorse, word for word, the address yesterday by Premier Molotoff. Adjustments must be made that will permit Germany and Poland to live side by side in peace.

I am resolved to fight until the Polish Government arrives at the decision that a solution can be attained. I want to eliminate the element of uncertainty between Poland and Germany.

PROMISES BOMB FOR BOMB

I do not want to fight women and children. The Poles have shot regular soldiers upon our territory, and from now on bomb will be met by bomb. He who fights with poison will be met with poison. He who departs from the rules of humane warfare can expect the same from us.

I shall carry on thus, fighting until the situation is acceptable to Germany.

For the last few years more than 90,000,000,000 marks have been applied to the reconstruction of the German Army. We have the best-equipped army. It is much better than the army of 1914.

If I now call upon the German people to make sacrifices I have a right to do so. I am ready to make every personal sacrifice on my own part. I expect nothing from any German but what I also would do myself and would always be prepared to do. My life belongs to my people. I shall march as the first German soldier of the people.

I have put on my old soldier's coat, and I will not take it off until we achieve victory.

If anything happens to me, then there shall come Marshal Goering. And if to Marshal Goering, then shall come Herr Hess. You shall be duty bound to them as you have been lo me.

In case something happens to take away Herr Hess, the choice shall be by the German people.

My whole life has been nothing but one long struggle, and there is one word I never learned to know: that is "capitulate." November of 1918 shall never be repeated in the history of Germany.

As long as I am willing to sacrifice my life for the German people, then the German people should do the same. If not, then they should be branded as traitors.

You [members of the Reichstag] are responsible for the sentiment in your districts and individual groups throughout the country. I expect discipline from the German women, too, in this struggle. We stand together. We will meet all obstacles. If your will is strong enough, then 23 cannot fail. Sieg Heil!

After the resolution to incorporate Danzig in the Reich [it was adopted unanimously] Marshal Goering spoke to the Reichstag. He said the German people would stand by the Chancellor to a man. They are resolved, he said, to bring his aims to pass as he stands behind the people.

"We expect you to do your duty to the utmost," said Marshal Goering. "We shall fight to the bitter end against the Poles."

Marshal Goering then proposed the following resolution:

"The Reich promises to stand behind the Fuehrer." That was acclaimed by "Deutschland Uber Alles," ending the session.

Hitler Is Already Creating New Wars of Tomorrow

BY ANNE O'HARE MCCORMICK | SEPT. 18, 1939

THE INVASION OF POLAND by Russian troops answers one fateful question. The agreement between Hitler and Stalin is not a mere non-aggression pact. It is a deal for joint action, a hands-across-the-Poles partnership for sharing the profits of the German conquest. Hopes that the Kremlin might be playing another double game, this time against Berlin, flickered when the armistice was signed which enabled Japan to get on with her business in China. They are extinguished as the Soviet forces move west. The sequel on two continents demonstrates that the Nazi-Soviet pact amounts to a permit for aggression.

From the flat, forlorn prairie on one side of the frontier, the Red Army has now marched into the equally flat and featureless plain on the other. Along the vague borderlands on the Polish side, particularly in the eastern sections of the provinces of Volhynia and Polesie, live the poorest and most primitive peasants in Poland. According to information gathered by the writer in Lwów last Spring, they are without Ukrainian national consciousness and incline toward Russia and communism. These are the people the Soviet Union, in its new concern for oppressed minorities, proposes to "protect" and incorporate.

FIRST NEUTRAL TO ENTER

Nevertheless, the unmarked boundary between the two countries and the two systems constitutes a spiritual borderline that has held for twenty years. In crossing it now Russia changes her role from that of passive to active participant in a widening conflict. While protesting "neutrality" — timely portent of the elasticity of that word of many meanings — she becomes the first of the great neutrals to enter the war. By violating Polish integrity she is technically at war with Britain and France. In ordering his troops to step out of Soviet territory,

Stalin does what informed observers predicted he would not dare to do. He does it in collusion with Nazi Germany. The Red Army invades Europe at the invitation of Adolf Hitler, the man who rose to power and arrived at the gates of Poland as the arch-enemy of Stalin and the protector of Germany and Europe against bolshevism.

This is the important fact. It proves that Hitler had to pay a heavy price to get his way in Poland. If Stalin exacted a part of the country to protect Russia against the German drive into the Ukraine and to make sure that Moscow as well as Berlin will delimit and share control of the rump State that will separate the two, it means that Hitler has surrendered his liberty of action as Mussolini surrendered his when he acquiesced in the seizure of Austria that brought Germany to the Brenner.

It is true that the crushing of Poland and the partnership with Russia, by increasing the terror in the neighboring States and reducing the value of the British guarantee, fortify Hitler in his designs on Rumania and Hungary. But it is also true that while he can hold Russian invasion of Bessarabia as a threat over Rumania, he can no longer move there or anywhere else in Central Europe except in agreement with Moscow. Since the last war the influence of Russia has been nil in a region where formerly she was always in, the way of German and Austrian plans for expansion. Now Hitler has drawn the old enemy back into Mitteleuropa, introduced a new competitor into the German "living room."

A WAVERING BATTLE LINE

The Russian-German line cutting through Poland is ominous but wavering. It wavers because not even Stalin or Hitler can ever be sure what goes on in the mind of the other. It was formed in the first place, one suspects, by a reckless desire to gloat over Britain and France. In their lofty enclosures, all dictators develop a gargantuan childishness very like that of the wicked giants in old fairy tales. They like to clank and "throw scares." Their attitude toward opposition is, "I'll show them!" No one is more taken in than they by their own "coups de théâtre."

Between the new line and the western front swing Turkey and Italy, one hitherto linked with Russia, the other with Germany, but both thrown out of alignment by juncture of Nazis and Soviets, As the result of Russia's practical abandonment of neutrality, they are the most important "neutrals" left in Europe, and their interdependent attitude is a relatively bigger factor in the balance. Turkey begins to tremble. Will Italy be more impressed or frightened by the shadow-alliance hanging over her?

One thing above all must strike the American observer as the new combine blasts at the remnants of the Versailles structure and we debate our attitude toward a crumbling Europe. Hitler set out to tear up the war treaties because they chained Germany and perpetuated the injustices of the status quo. Most liberals agreed that the post-war edifice could not endure. But if that is true, look at his substitute. What chance of survival has the prison house of conquered nations he is clamping together?

Hitler is not only making war today; he is creating the wars of tomorrow. Unshackled, he is undermining the last pillars of the temple and filling it with hates that only greater destruction will assuage. Senator Vandenberg is right in saying that twenty years ago we did not win a war to end wars; but Hitler has let loose a war to begin all wars.

Hitler Is Insane, Specialist Holds

BY THE NEW YORK TIMES | OCT. 20, 1939

LONDON, OCT. 19 — Dr. William Brown, director of the Institute of Experimental Psychology at Oxford University and a world authority on diseases of the mind, has completed years of study of the character and mentality of Adolf Hitler, with the conclusion that the German Chancellor is suffering from a chronic form of insanity, known as paranoia, that will gradually impair his intellect until he destroys himself or becomes a raving maniac.

In a letter to The Times of London, which he later expanded in a talk with this correspondent, Dr. Brown, who was Terry lecturer at Yale University in 1927 and 1928 and who has contributed a psychological treatise to the Encyclopedia Britannica, explained:

> Sir Nevile Henderson's final report on the actions of Herr Hitler confirms my conclusion, reached six months ago, that he has every symptom of the paranoiac who is suffering from persecutory mania and whose brainstorms and megalomania will increase until his madness is so apparent that he must be isolated.

"HYSTERICAL TENDENCY" FOUND

Dr. Brown says the following tendencies are definite ingredients in the German Chancellor's mental make-up:

> First, a hysterical tendency, shown in his emotional appeal to crowds in which his mind seems to undergo temporary dissociation through the very intensity of his concentration upon the matter in hand. With his mind so narrowed down on one point he may be temporarily oblivious of other considerations and thus may appear perfidious. There is also a probable hysterical identification in subconscious fantasy with Frederick the Great and a tendency toward mechanical imitation of the less admirable political manoeuvres of him and of Napoleon, which makes him appear, judged by modern standards, as an atavistic monster.

Second, a paranoid tendency amounting almost to persecutory mania. He is a very aggressive person and projects this aggressiveness upon the world around him, being acutely on guard against aggression from others with the suspicion, and possibly delusions, that such hostile aggressiveness is active against himself and his nation.

Third, a growing megalomania with Messianic feelings. This is a further development of his paranoid tendency, making his followers paranoid and producing collective paranoia.

Fourth, a compulsive tendency — in his case a power impulse — toward more and more bloodless victories in which his latest claim to territory or power is called his last — like the alcoholic who calls his latest drink his last.

EXPLANATION OF SOVIET FACT

Dr. Brown submits that this analysis explains at least in part the German Chancellor's astonishing volte-face in signing up with Joseph Stalin, whom he had vilified for years.

"After the events of last March," the psychologist wrote to The Times, "Herr Hitler's paranoid fear of encirclement became so intense and his accompanying aggressiveness so magnified that the unbearable mental tension could only be relieved by a retreat to Moscow."

Again and again the psychologist went back to Sir Nevile Henderson's description in his reports as British Ambassador in Berlin — now published by the government — of the wild scenes at the Berlin chancellory when, as Sir Nevile wrote, "Herr Hitler was in a mood of extreme excitability" and his language was "violent, recriminatory and exaggerated." These descriptions, Dr. Brown says, read like one of his own reports on a typical case of a paranoiac.

There is little chance, in Dr, Brown's view, that Herr Hitler's "disease" will bring about an early breakdown, though it may if Germany is being pressed in the field, resulting in the necessity for many terrible decisions. Dr. Brown believes the history of the world in recent years would have been entirely different if Herr Hitler had led a normal life.

"In Freud's view," Dr. Brown said, "all paranoiacs were homosexual, but in Herr Hitler's case this, in recent years, apparently has been repressed, and today all manifestation of love is self-love and love of Germany."

This love of Germany, Dr. Brown explains, is so great that the Chancellor thinks in an entirely different way from a normal human being. Thus he cannot understand why the Allies do not trust him, even after he has repeatedly broken his promise, and thus he was surprised, as Sir Nevile Henderson reported, when the world was shocked by his march into Prague last March.

Dr. Brown believes Herr Hitler's condition is partly due to heredity and partly to his lonely early days in Vienna. The psychologist has studied Herr Hitler's family history and he believes there is a paranoid tendency there too. He explains that Herr Hitler's "mother fixation" was the first sign of his abnormality and he has discovered some other undisclosed facts about the life of the Chancellor that, he says, help explain the tragedy of the man and the present war in Europe.

Seven Years of Hitler

BY THE NEW YORK TIMES | JAN. 29, 1940

TOMORROW is a fateful anniversary. On Jan, 30, seven years ago, the aging President von Hindenburg appointed Adolf Hitler Chancellor of Germany at the head of a coalition Cabinet. The Reichstag fire, the dictatorship and concentration camps, the rearmament and imperial conquests of the next seven years were still to come; but all over Germany the Brown Shirts exulted. Endless columns of them swung through the Brandenburg Gate in Berlin holding torches that heightened the blood-red of their swastika banners. The crowds were ecstatic; the Brown Shirts were sure that their moment of history had come. How well they knew!

Outside Germany — and inside it too — democratic leaders did not know what was happening, and did not care to know. Paris, as usual, was in the throes of a Cabinet crisis; a young Radical named Edouard Daladier was chosen as Premier. London felt some misgivings, but looked upon Hitler as a bizarre adventurer who would be tamed by the responsibilities of office. Washington was struggling with the depression at home and absorbed in war debt discussions abroad. Wall Street took the news from Berlin calmly. We were told, even from Berlin, that Hitler was a "prisoner of the Right" who would not be allowed to carry out his program. Industrialists in Germany looked at the reassuring Prussian features of Alfred Hugenberg, their representative and spokesman in the new Cabinet, and felt confident that Hitler would do his bidding and theirs. It was fashionable to predict that Hitler would "blow up" within a few months, now that he had passed at last from agitation to action.

From these tragically mistaken judgments of 1933 we can understand, to some extent, how Hitler was able to paralyze Europe with fear and at length grip it by the throat in 1939. "Mein Kampf" was 10 years old when he first came to power. His record was known, his ambitions of limitless power were publicly avowed. Unlike others who have aspired to world conquest, he was cynical enough to show his blueprint to the world. In Europe and America there were students of German affairs who saw the man as a portent and a peril; their warnings were disregarded. Apparent for all to see in 1933 was the economic and spiritual sickness in Germany that was to lead so quickly to the mental breakdown of a great people; yet nothing effective had been done to help in the days of Bruening, when there might still have been time.

Likewise the terrifying implications of a Hitler as leader of 70 million Germans were not faced at the time, or for years afterward. The British did not really comprehend them until the ultimatum of Godesberg, in the Munich crisis of 1938; and even then they hoped, for six months more, that something would "turn up." It was so much easier for British and French statesmen to assure their publics that all would be well, to trust in Hitler's soothing deceptions and ignore the menace in his party and his program. The influence of Mr. Micawber on democratic foreign policy was not the least of the factors which enabled the Cabinet "prisoner" of January, 1933, to engulf Europe in war six and a half years later.

When at last this latest of Europe's recurrent challenges by a military adventurer is defeated, whole peoples will be weary. There will be a desperate longing in all countries to slide back into the peace and quiet of happier days. Politicians, sensing the public mood, will no doubt be able to win elections again with a cry of "normalcy" as we heard it in 1920, or of "tranquillity," as the British listened to it in 1922. Mental indolence is always at a premium after an exhausting war; and it will be so pleasant again, not only in our own fortunate country but in the surviving democracies of Western Europe, to ignore disagreeable facts abroad and concentrate solely on internal affairs. But the career of Hitler has shown in seven short years that social improvement, cultural advancement, material happiness for millions upon millions of "little men" can be shattered by one fanatical leader who is not watched in time.

Nazis Rate Hitler a Military Genius

BY THE NEW YORK TIMES | APRIL 21, 1940

BERLIN, APRIL 20 — The appearance of cheering hundreds in the Wilhelmsplatz before the Reich's Chancellory and the flapping of flags in the sunshine were the only outward signs of observance of Adolf Hitler's fifty-first birthday today.

Germany, in accordance with what was said to have been Herr Hitler's wish, passed the day without large-scale celebrations of any kind. The outstanding birthday present was a collection of war-material metal that Field Marshal Hermann Goering formally presented to the Chancellor in the morning.

The German press described the drive for the collection as an "overwhelming success" without mentioning the amount of metal collected. Amateur statisticians figure that if every man, woman and child in the country donated two pounds the volume would amount to about 80,000 tons, or enough to fill 2,000 German freight cars and make a train 12 miles long, As collections were also made in the Protectorate of Bohemia-Moravia and in the former Polish territories, the total is probably greater than that.

Birthday comment in the press makes a point of Herr Hitler's qualities, not so much as leader of the nation but as a military genius. Dr. Robert Ley, head of the Labor Front, writing in the Angriff, says:

> It is a long way from the former lance corporal of the World War to supreme commander of the world's largest and most dependable army. This ascension of a simple soldier within twenty years is unique in history.
>
> This time we will win the battles and the war, for we will have the last battalions in the field. Adolf Hitler, soldier and military leader, is our guarantee for this.

WEST FRONT PUTS ON SHOW

The soldiers on the Western Front, according to reports here, celebrated Herr Hitler's birthday with more display. Signal lights were set off as fireworks and searchlights were played on banners having slogans such as "We congratulate our Fuehrer," and "Onward to victory with the Fuehrer."

At one point, it is reported, when near midnight the Rhine Valley was suddenly lit up by dozens of white signal lights, the French artillery opened a sporadic fire.

In a brief silence between bursts the German troops started singing Reich anthems. The sound of their voices wafted across the river, it is stated, quieted the French fears of an attack and the firing soon ceased.

In the capital the forenoon conference of the military leaders with Herr Hitler at the Chancellory was interrupted briefly when best wishes for the occasion were voiced to their Supreme Commander by Col. Gen. Walter von Brauchitsch, the Commander in Chief of the army; Marshal Goering and Grand Admiral Erich Raeder, the head of the navy.

Toward noon the heads of the Reich Ministries, National Socialist party leaders and other high officials congratulated the Chancellor, while the noise of the cheering people outside filtered through the windows.

Herr Hitler made his first public appearance of the day on the balcony of the Chancellory about 1:30 P. M. During the rest of the day he appeared from time to time and waved his hand to the crowd.

The buildings of the foreign diplomatic missions, including the American Embassy, flew the flags of their nations at the behest of the Papal Nuncio, who is dean of the diplomatic corps. Late in the day the diplomatic chiefs called at the Chancellery and signed their names in the register, the American Charge d'Affaires, Alexander Kirk, representing the United States at this function.

Marshal Goering, in an address broadcast to the men and women in German industry, emphasized that the duties facing them in wartime were doubly important.

Nazi World Revolution Is Hitler's Objective

BY OTTO D. TOLISCHUS | MAY 12, 1940

STOCKHOLM, SWEDEN, MAY 11 — Casting the warnings of his generals to the winds and putting everything on one card, Adolf Hitler, master of 80,000,000 Germans and 30,000,000 conquered subject peoples, has now started his long-awaited and oft-postponed offensive in the West. He has assumed supreme command and therewith personal responsibility for a campaign that will decide not only his fate and that of his regime, but also, in the words of his own proclamation, "the fate of the German people for the next 1,000 years."

Never before has the Western world faced so mighty an enemy or so fundamental an issue. Never before has Germany herself been faced so categorically with the alternative of world power or downfall.

LAST WAR AND THIS

In a military sense, this war, after its episodical preliminaries, starts like the World War in the classical German tradition with a vast flanking movement through the Low Countries in which this time not only Belgium but also the Netherlands is involved. But in every other respect, especially in causes, aims and methods, it differs from all other European wars since the fall of the Roman Empire.

Contrary to much current American opinion, this war is no longer a game of power politics between grasping nations of the wicked Old World. It is by proclamation of the National Socialist regime itself a revolutionary war — a war that heralds a world revolution in which are to be laid the new foundations for the twentieth century and the next millennium.

The question is not, as it was even in the World War, which nation shall be first in a Europe that is a fundamentally constituted and ideological entity with common morals, common aspirations and a common way of life. The question is whether Europe and the world shall preserve their present social, political and economic structure or whether they shall change to a radically different one.

"HERALD OF REVOLUTION"

For this war, by the proclamation of the National Socialist regime itself, is a revolutionary war — a war that heralds a world revolution in which are to be laid the new foundations for the twentieth century and the next millennium. It is being fought in the name of the new revolutionary ideology, which seeks to assert itself over what it regards as the *ancien régime.*

This is a revolution as fundamental as the French Revolution, whose generating ideas had also given birth to the American Revolution and which finally ended in the Napoleonic Wars. And being a revolution, it has developed its own fanatic revolutionary faith, which finds adherents even in the enemy camp and against which a mere revival of the shop-worn slogans of the last war falls short of success.

In its essence, this new ideology is the very antithesis of the French Revolution. Then it was liberalism and individualism breaking the bonds of feudalism and the autocracy of kings. Now the pendulum is swinging back again. A generation associated with individualism, whose loss it never suffered, and weary of personal responsibilities and economic difficulties, seeks refuge in a new collectivism. This collectivism, whether based on class or race, has one prerequisite to its success. It must be based on iron discipline and an authoritarian regime that coolly sacrifices the individual for the benefit of the collective whole, even if in practice this means for the benefit of the ruling caste.

In practice, National Socialist collectivism is predicated on new political and economic organizations.

In its political concepts this collectivism harks back on the one hand to the mystic German ideal of the Reich — the Holy Roman Empire of German nationality, as the universal empire of Christendom. On the other hand, it goes back to the ideal propounded by Napoleon in his self-created legend of a continental European consolidation against Great Britain. The ideal of "the Reich" is a favorite topic of German press discussion.

NAPOLEON'S IDEA BORROWED

The Napoleonic concept was propounded by Chancellor Hitler himself in his speech of Jan. 30, 1940, in which he said:

For 300 years England pursued the aim of preventing a real consolidation of Europe, just as France sought for centuries to prevent a consolidation of Germany.

The consolidation of the German people, which was Herr Hitler's first aim, was achieved in the Munich settlement that ended Richelieu's political maxims, which had dominated French policy since his time. Now the German armies are marching in the name of European consolidation against the British Empire. And Alfred Rosenberg already proclaims:

Germany has become the protector of the endangered and oppressed continent. It is fighting against an unholy division of the old and venerable European continent into dozens of pigmy States. National Socialist Germany, the heart of Central Europe, enters upon its historic rights.

As the German press puts it, "the German epoch has begun and the history of Europe will again be primarily a German history."

To think that all this conflicts with the seemingly exclusive German racial doctrine is an optical illusion which long deceived the world. For while this doctrine asserts the rights of the German "master race," it also makes the "race" or "folk" and not the State the unit of political organization, which can take many forms.

Therewith it sets aside the ideal of the national State that ruled the nineteenth century. It opens the way for the establishment of many "folk organizations" that can range from the Polish Gouvernement General and the Jewish reservation in it to the Bohemian-Moravian

Protectorate and the Slovak and Danish garrison States with local cultural self-administration, but under the complete economic and political domination of Germany.

Extend that system throughout Europe and allot to the various nations their respective "folk organizations" according to the precedents already applied to those who resisted and those who did not resist, and the picture of the "new Europe" in its "consolidated" state begins to take form.

At the same time the racial doctrine, though wide enough for a supernational empire, still calls for a German kernel state inhabited by Germans alone who, when they need more room by virtue of their biological potency, annex to their own state not merely population but land from which the alien population is removed.

In the matter of economic organization, the National Socialist collectivism propounds a national and an international "socialism" that is based on a national and an international planned economy or Grossraumwirtschaft, for which the whole continent is to form the Grosswirtschaftsraum and in which "labor," not gold, is to provide the measure of value and therewith the basis of the currency.

BASIS OF REORGANIZATION

In this supernational economy the various national economies would be reorganized according to their best separate capacities to supplement one another, but above all to supply German economy with what it needs: that is, principally food and raw materials. The "labor currency" would naturally give quite a different valuation to the per hour work unit of the German worker than to that of a Balkan peasant.

If that sounds complicated, it is merely necessary to keep in mind that the German currency already possesses an artificial "managed" value that determines the price of German goods and therewith their international exchange value, and it can be adjusted at will.

It is in this sense that National Socialism has proclaimed a war against the "plutocracies," against the "tyranny of gold" and against free world trade.

Thus what was likely shoved aside a few short years ago as fanatic Nazi propaganda is now assuming the contours of a very realistic program. And the roles to be allotted to various other "folk" in the "new Europe" are already being enacted by the Czechs, the Poles, the Slovaks, the Danes and the Norwegians, not to mention the Jews.

In the words of Arthur Greiser, Danzig gauleiter, "only great nations with a high Kultur are called to leadership; small nations are useful only under the protection and leadership of great nations."

OBSTACLES TO SUCCESS

At the same time, despite German successes hitherto, there remain many obstacles to the realization of this program. The first are France and Great Britain, with their political democracy and free economy, backed by a military force that is holding Germany at bay. But the issue between them is already joined in battle, in which victory or defeat depends on whether the German air force or what Herr Hitler once called "England's scrap-iron navy" proves its superiority. And that issue no man can foretell.

But, even assuming German victory, it appears inevitable that in such a case the present war would be only one of a series as prolonged, perhaps, as were the Napoleonic Wars, for such a victory would be won by an alliance of three dictators whose programs are so all-embracing and dynamic that there is not room enough in Europe for all three. After the elimination of their joint opposition, they would have to proceed on eliminating one another.

And if, in such an elimination contest, National Socialist Germany comes out on top and organizes Europe according to her heart's desire, there still remains the fact that even a Europe thus organized would be far from self-sufficient. Economic necessities alone would compel an extension of its control.

COLONIES IN SCHEME

And therein, again, lie all hopes for a National Socialist world revolution. For the masters of Europe may be expected to assume control and to coordinate in their systems the vast European colonies and dominions overseas which, barring the American position, cover much of Asia and all of Africa and Australia.

Beyond that the exponents of that revolution are convinced that the economic weight of a consolidated Europe alone is too great for the rest of the world to ignore without an economic and therewith social, political catastrophe. And since such a Europe would dictate its own terms of economic intercourse, the rest of the world would have to conform by adopting the same methods.

Herr Hitler Rewrites
Military Story of 1918

BY EDWIN L. JAMES | JUNE 23, 1940

IN HANDING HIS armistice terms to the French, Adolf Hitler repeated the story of which he has been so fond, namely that the German Army was not defeated in 1918 but was tricked into surrender. The preamble to the terms said that at the end of the World War the Reich had not been beaten, that the Germans showed only one weakness, "belief in the promise of democratic statesmen." Germany had trusted in the Fourteen Points of President Wilson and had been cheated — that was the story.

Having said this over and over for the past seven years and more, Hitler may believe it. Psychologists tell us that a man may repeat a lie so often that he becomes convinced it is true. But because Hitler may believe it does not make it true. Germany was not tricked in the Fall of 1918. Germany was defeated. Had she not been defeated she would have paid no attention at all to Wilson's Fourteen Points. She had to surrender and Wilson's program was simply the straw at which she grasped.

Here is the record as Hitler writes it:

In reliance on assurance given to the German Reich by the American President Wilson and confirmed by the Allied Powers, German armed forces laid down their arms in November, 1918.

Therewith was ended a war which the German people and its government had not wanted and in which the enemy, despite tremendous superiority, did not successfully in any way conquer the German Army, Navy or German Air Force.

WHAT THE RECORD SHOWS

Over against Hitler's case, let the position be stated as follows: In the

Fall of 1918, the German armies were beaten in a war which started when the Kaiser invaded Belgium more than four years previously. The German armies were tired and faced with dismay the growing size of the United States forces entering the battle line in France. At home morale had broken down, revolution was rife and Germany had to quit. The Allied blockade had had much to do with dissatisfaction back of the German lines, and this breaking down of esprit had spread to the fighting forces. The very commanders of the German Army were the first to advise surrender.

That is, admittedly, a different story from that told by Hitler.

Let us look at the record.

In the last days of the World War, the commander of the German forces was General Eric Ludendorff; Hitler was an infantry corporal. Interestingly enough, five years after the end of the war, when Hitler was starting the National Socialist movement, Ludendorff cooperated with him. They were both mixed up in the ill-fated Munich putsch of 1923, after which Ludendorff went into retirement and Hitler went to jail. That was when he wrote "Mein Kampf." But, be that as it may, it is fair to assume that the Generalissimo knew more about the military situation of the German armies in the Fall of 1918 than did the corporal.

What did the Generalissimo have to say about it ?

THE REPORT OF LUDENDORFF

Fortunately for the record, Ludendorff wrote his story in two volumes, which were published in 1919. The English translation was printed by Harper & Brothers.

Picking up Ludendorff's story in July of 1918, we find this paragraph on Page 323 of Vol. ii:

> The effort to make the nations of the Entente inclined to peace before the arrival of the American reinforcements by means of German victories had failed. The energy of the army had not sufficed to deal the enemy a decisive blow before the Americans were on the spot in considerable

force. It was quite clear to me that our general situation had thus become very serious.

On Aug. 8 there came the attacks of the British and French armies which caused Ludendorff to say, on Page, 326 Vol. ii: "Aug. 8 was the black day of the German Army in the history of this war." Two pages farther he recorded: "By the early hours of the forenoon of Aug. 8 I had already gained a complete impression of the situation. It was a very gloomy one. ... The situation was uncommonly serious."

And then on Page 332: "The fate of the German people was to me too high a stake. The war must be ended."

WHEN WILHELM GAVE UP

On Page 333 of Vol. ii Ludendorff reported: "The Emperor told me later that after the failure of the July offensive and after Aug. 8 he knew the war could no longer be won."

It was then recorded, Page 335, Vol. ii, that on Aug. 14 the Kaiser instructed Secretary of State von Hintze to institute peace negotiations, if possible through the Queen of Holland.

After a long review of the military situation in which emphasis was laid on the lack of morale among the civil population, which, he said was spreading to the troops, Ludendorff said the military situation was becoming worse and worse. On Page 372 he wrote: "In these circumstances I felt compelled to undertake the responsible task of hastening the end of the war." He reported that nothing had come of the Kaiser's project to approach the Queen of Holland.

On Page 376 Ludendorff told of a conference with Hindenberg on Sept. 28 when he said the Field Marshal agreed with him that Germany must ask for a cessation of fighting. Then comes on Page 378 the first mention of Wilson. In the presence of Hindenburg and Ludendorff, von Hintze suggested an approach to Wilson, of whose high ideals he had heard, and on Sept. 29 it was decided to send a note to Wilson, and a copy of it to the British and French, after the Kaiser had agreed to this procedure. It was sent on Oct. 5.

HOW THE WAR ENDED

On Oct. 2 Major Baron von dem Bussche, as an envoy of Ludendorff, addressed the Reichstag and delivered the message that Germany must stop fighting. In his address he said: "We must, accordingly, lose no time. Every twenty-four hours that pass may make our position worse and give the enemy a clearer view of our present weakness."

The next day a new German Government was formed, headed by Prince Max of Baden. Almost immediately there was placed before it a report from von Hindenburg which concluded by saying: "In these circumstances the only right course is to give up the fight in order to spare useless sacrifices for the German people and their allies. Every day wasted costs the lives of thousands of brave German soldiers."

Ludendorff then told at length of the criticism which arose against him after the armistice negotiations had passed from the military to the civilian authorities. He rested on his statement that Germany had been defeated arid could not go on fighting, although he found the terms, as they materialized, very severe. By Oct. 24 both he and Hindenburg were advising rejection of the Wilson terms. But, as Ludendorff said: "In the note of Oct. 27 we capitulated." Two days later Ludendorff resigned.

The concluding chapter of Ludendorff's book is given over to a description of the German revolution which broke out on Nov. 9. He felt that Germany was gone as a nation.

In a final sentence he wrote: "After our great fall, let us learn once again to be Germans, and to be proud that we are Germans. God grant it!"

But the record he penned stands. It shows that Germany was defeated on the field of battle. Now Hitler finds that never happened.

Herr Hitler's tale is not baloney; it is wurst.

Hitler Welcomed by Frenzied Berlin

BY PERCIVAL KNAUTH | JULY 7, 1940

BERLIN, JULY 6 — Adolf Hitler, "field lord," "guider of battles," "victor of the greatest campaign in history" rode triumphant into Berlin today over a carpet of flowers.

The mile-long route from the Anhalter station to the Chancellery was a perfumed avenue of greens, reds, blues and yellows flanked by cheering thousands who shouted and wept themselves into a frantic hysteria as the Fuehrer passed.

Whatever price in misery and sorrow Germany paid for her defeat 22 years ago was forgotten today in the frenzied joy of victory. Caesar in his glory was never more turbulently received and Adolf Hitler, one-time corporal in the Kaiser's army, was indeed accorded a Caesar's welcome.

Eight weeks of warfare, moreover, had changed him. The spirit that had animated him to snap his fingers in glee when he received the news that the French had asked for an armistice was evident today in the beaming smiles and the frank delight he showed at his reception.

He was greeted at the station by Field Marshal Hermann Goering and nearly every military government and party functionary of high rank in the Reich.

Dr. Hjalmar Schacht, former President of the Reichsbank, who recently has been rarely seen at official public receptions, was present, sharing a car with Dr. Alfred Rosenberg, director of Nazi ideological training. Nazi district leaders from every German province had traveled to Berlin to meet him.

Outside the station in the hot sun milling thousands jammed the streets for blocks while white-bloused Hitler Maidens strewed his path with Summer flowers till the gray surface disappeared under the many-colored carpet.

The special Hitler train, drawn by two flag-bedecked locomotives, guarded by two cars of anti-aircraft artillery, entered the Anhalter station at 3 o'clock this afternoon. As it stopped before the red-carpeted platform, fanfares of the Hitler Youth trumpeted his welcome, while all over Berlin bells rang out the news that "the victor has come home."

A Storm Troopers' brass band swung into the Badenweiler March as the Fuehrer stepped down from the train and shook hands with Marshal Goering, who has become slimmer and healthier in the last two months. Foreign Minister Joachim von Ribbentrop and Col. Gen. Wilhelm Keitel, Chief of the Supreme Command of the Armed Forces, who had accompanied Herr Hitler on the train, followed as he passed slowly along the line of official welcomers, drawn up according to rank on the platform.

The shrill cheering of Hitler Youth and Hitler Maidens on the opposite platform was incessant. Though the train hid Herr Hitler from their view they shouted their young throats hoarse and as their "Heils" echoed down the vast arcade of the station the crowd outside took up the shout and passed the word along.

At the lower end of the platform lights were blazing from platforms high above. The doorway of the station was wreathed in greenery. Gold beribboned flags hung from walls. Everywhere there were pots of flowers.

MANY GUARDS HOLD CROWD

The balustrade of the stairs leading out to the street was intertwined with garlands of oak, symbolic of victory. Troopers of the armed Elite Guard stood at ramrod attention every three feet. Outside the guards holding back the crowds were in three lines with arms locked, straining to keep a clear path for the long line of official cars.

An honor company was drawn up before the Chancellery but Herr Hitler did not review it and drove on through the gates. A small body of wounded soldiers was lined up on the sidewalk before the entrance and as the car curved in from the street one of them ran up to grasp the Chancellor's extended hand.

The Chancellor twice appeared on the balcony of the Chancellery overlooking Wilhelmplatz, which was packed to the corners with men and women, many of whom had stood there since early morning. Marshal Goering. Col. Gen. Walther von Brauchitsch, army chief of staff; Grand Admiral Erich Raeder, Foreign Minister von Ribbentrop and Rudolf Hess, deputy leader of the Nazi party, appeared with him.

His attention was devoted more to them than to the crowd. He talked animatedly with them, laughing and digging them in the ribs. Only after several minutes did he turn to the crowd with smiles and waves of his hand.

The public celebration was cut short this time. Immediately after Herr Hitler's first appearance on the balcony loudspeakers admonished the crowds to disperse. "The Fuehrer will appear once more," it was announced. "He has important conferences and asks you all to go home."

Part of the crowd began to sing "We Are Sailing Against England," but the song quickly died as Herr Hitler, with Marshal Goering, appeared for the last time. He briefly waved and smiled and then disappeared. It was some time, however, in spite of repeated requests through the loudspeakers, before the crowd dispersed.

As darkness settled over the city the festive spirit that had, flourished in the sunlight waned under the sobering influence of the blackout, though there was a small group of Red Cross nurses and Labor Service Girls waiting before the Chancellery to catch another glimpse of the victorious Field Lord.

He Only Wanted To Be Liked

BY THE NEW YORK TIMES | SEPT. 6, 1940

ADOLF HITLER, as he stated in his latest speech in Berlin's Sportpalast, has been worrying because people who live outside the range of German guns don't like him. "We want to construct a new state," he complains. "Why do others hate us so?"

We can only say that in his modest and diffident way he did not court popularity. He did not win the approval of those who believe in free institutions when he used a minority party to trick the German people out of their liberties; when he abolished opposition parties; when he outlawed German citizens of Jewish faith or origin; when he persecuted Protestants and Catholics for preferring God to himself; when he imprisoned, silenced, killed or drove into exile all of Germany's creative minds; when he completed the conquest of a country not his own by butchering a considerable number of his own followers.

He did not seem lovable when he promised to respect Austrian sovereignty and broke that promise; promised to respect Czech sovereignty and broke that promise; made a treaty with Poland and bombed her cities, stole her territory and suppressed her independence; denounced the Communists as the scum of the earth and then made an amicable *plunderbund* with them; promised lasting peace at Munich and tore up that promise a year later; invaded Denmark, Norway, Holland, Luxembourg and Belgium without provocation; sent his airmen to bomb and machine-gun helpless old men, women and children fleeing from the violated regions.

He has not endeared himself on this side of the water by sending his agents to stir up trouble and dissension, openly in Latin America, more furtively in this country; by making it evident that wherever in the world a dirty or brutal deed was to be done he would do it, encourage it or endorse it; by sending at the head of his bleak cavalry the four horsemen of ignorance, prejudice, tyranny and death.

Perhaps he only wanted to be liked. Let it rest at that. He isn't.

Hitler Forswears 'Any Compromise'

BY PERCIVAL KNAUTH | NOV. 9, 1940

BERLIN, NOV. 8 — Before the traditional gathering of Nazi "old fighters" in Munich's Loewenbrau Keller on the eve of the seventeenth anniversary of his beer hall Putsch, Reichsfuehrer Adolf Hitler tonight reaffirmed his "absolute conviction" in the ultimate triumph of German arms.

He defied the world, stating that today there was no combination of powers that could equal the resources and the might of Germany and her allies.

Emphasizing his "unalterable determination to continue the struggle to a clear decision," he declared:

"Today I reject any compromise."

Herr Hitler delivered his speech with fire and vigor and was unsparing in his caustic denunciation of Great Britain as the seeker of war. It was a warlike pronouncement, delivered to military men, The hall was crowded with the field gray uniforms of "old fighters," released from active service for the celebration, as well as high military officials of today present as guests of Herr Hitler.

Herr Hitler for the first time on such an occasion was in the field gray uniform of Supreme Field Lord. The meeting took place this time in the Loewenbrau Keller, since the famous Buergerbraeu Keller, burned a year ago when a bomb exploded just after Herr Hitler had left, has not been restored.

No such incident marred tonight's meeting. The Loewenbrau Keller decorated with swastika flags, resounded again and again with the cheers with which the "old fighters" greeted their leader's words.

He described himself as "one of the hardest men Germany has had for decades, perhaps for centuries, equipped with the greatest authority of any German leader."

"But above all," he stated, "I believe in my success. I believe in it unconditionally. I am firmly convinced that this struggle will not end differently by a single hair than the struggle that I once waged in Germany itself.

I am convinced that Providence has brought me this far and has spared me from all the dangers in order to let me lead the German people in this battle.

"I participated in the great war," he recalled. "I belong to those who then were cheated of their success. It is therefore my unshakable determination that this struggle shall not end as did that one."

Recapitulating German history since 1914, Herr Hitler described the World War as "a war that Germany did not want."

Germany was "poorly armed" when that war broke out, he said, "but she held for four years."

"For four years they [the Allies] strained themselves," he went on, "and then they had to get the American magician-priest, who found a formula that took in the German nation, trusting in the word of honor of a foreign President."

He described the growth of the Nazi party in the years before and after the Munich Putsch of 1923; He flung words of heavy sarcasm against Jews, bitter words against democratic regimes.

PREPARED TO MAKE PEACE

But he said that if Germany were able to pay 5,000,000,000 marks in reparations, "then we can also spend 5,000,000,000 internally for reparations."

Reaffirming that "I was prepared to make peace," he continued:

If England had agreed, good. They did not agree. Also good.

But then no compromises; nothing done by halves. I decided that either we were no soldiers or else we were the best in the world.

He described the increase in German production under his economic and financial measures. He reiterated his peaceful aims at that time, stating:

You know the foreign political conception I had in those days. I wanted the closest friendship with England. I thought the Germanic races should go together.

I wanted the same relationship with Italy. I also thought of Japan as a power with whose interests our own could coincide.

Both with Italy — and here he expressed his respect for Premier Mussolini — and with Japan he had succeeded, he said, "but unfortunately it did not succeed with England, contrary to our own wishes."

He reminded his listeners of the post-Munich days and said:

Then came the moment when it was no longer a question of whether war could be avoided entirely, but only if it could be avoided for one or two or three years by means of very serious German humiliations. At the moment when I realized that England wanted only to gain time, that over there they were determined under any circumstances to wage war with us, in that same moment I had only one wish:

If they were determined to declare war on us, then I hoped they would do it while I was still alive.

"WILL ORGANIZE EUROPE"

The war, he said, had turned out differently from what the Axis's enemies had expected. Germany and Italy, he asserted, would now organize Europe.

"If England says that the war will continue," he declared, "that is all the same to me. But it will end with our victory. You may believe me in that."

Summarizing the first year of the war, he described German losses as scarcely more than half of those in the Franco-Prussian War of 1870. Materially, he said, the German Army had used in ammunition only part of the monthly production of German arms factories. German reserves were so huge, Herr Hitler added, that he had had to curtail production; transferring it to "other fields, where I believe we must be especially strong."

After speaking sarcastically of the production figures aimed at in Australia and Canada, he declared:

As far as American production figures are concerned, they cannot even be formulated in astronomical figures. In this field, therefore, I do not want to be a competitor. But I can assure you of one thing: German production capacity is the highest in the world. And we will not climb down from it, because we are in a position today to mobilize the power of almost all Europe — and that I shall do so industrially you may well believe.

PRODUCTION HELD GROWING

Germany's material production, Herr Hitler continued, now was only growing. "We are prepared for the future," he stated emphatically, "better than ever before." As to Germany's present position, he stated:

Germany today, in any case, is together with her Allies and strong enough to oppose any combination of powers in the world. There is no coalition of powers that could equal ours.

He dwelt lengthily on the air war, telling how he had "waited three months" before "accepting the battle" proffered by the R. A. F. British bombs, he stated, could only increase Germany's determination.

As to peace, he declared that "it is my unalterable determination to carry the conflict on to a clear decision."

Just as I, as a National Socialist, declined all compromise in the battle for Germany, I today refuse all compromise. Some one must break, and under no circumstances will it be Germany.

His concluding words were devoted to the memory of the victims of the march to Feldherrnhalle seventeen years ago. They, he said, like the Germans today, fought for a new Germany. "From this struggle," he said, "Germany will finally emerge."

Hitler Challenges World Democracy

BY C. BROOKS PETERS | DEC. 11, 1940

BERLIN, DEC. 10 — For 90 minutes this morning Adolf Hitler addressed workers of Germany gathered before radios at their places of work throughout the Reich. And when he had concluded his remarks the inescapable conclusion was that, in the opinion of the supreme leader of the German Reich, the only possible end to the present conflict between democratic capitalism and totalitarian "socialism" by the very nature of the struggle would have to be found in the vanquishment of one of the contending systems.

Herr Hitler spoke over a national hook-up from the assembly hall of the Rheinmetall Borsig munitions plant in a northern suburb of Berlin. He was surrounded by cannon in various stages of completion, and he faced that factory's 12,000 armament workers. He spoke in moderate tones and avoided any reference to whatever political or military plans his government might have in preparation.

Viewed in their entirety, Herr Hitler's noonday remarks to his followers seem to have been designed chiefly for home consumption. For he placed the greatest emphasis upon benefits that, he said, accrue to workers under the system of government of which he is the champion. At the same time he delivered a frontal attack on the faults that, he asserted, were inherent in the system represented and practiced by the Western democracies.

As outlined by Herr Hitler today, democracy is synonymous with oligarchy. Of Britain and America, he declared:

> *The people are not the focal point of consideration. Of decisive importance is the existence of a few hundred gigantic capitalists who are in possession of their factories and their stocks and who in the final analysis thus steer the people. The broad masses do not interest them in the least or, at most, only in times of election. Otherwise, the life of the broad masses is a matter of complete indifference to them.*

On the other hand, Herr Hitler asserted the National Socialist State labored for the best interest of all classes and that birth was no longer of any importance in ascending the highest positions in the Reich hierarchy. Using himself as example he declared, while his audience laughed its pleasure:

I am not even a lawyer, yet I am nevertheless your Fuehrer.

The highest places in the government, he added, are occupied by men who once were workers, and he said that in the army there were now thousands of officers who had risen from the ranks.

"We know exactly," Herr Hitler declared, "that if we are defeated in this battle it is the end. Not just of our socialistic work of construction, but the end of the German people."

At the same time the Reichsfuehrer said he well understood that the leaders of the democratic capitalistic system foresaw the end of their system should the idea that inspired the Third Reich prove victorious in the war now being waged.

"We find ourselves in the midst of a conflict in which more is at stake than the victory of one or another land," he declared. "It is truly a battle of two worlds against each other."

"STAND AGAINST THE WORLD"

"In this struggle," he added, "I stand against the world as the representative of the have-nots. I have never recognized the legal claims of others to that which they stole by force. In no case can I allow the justification of those legal claims for what has been taken from us "

"There are two worlds that stand opposed to each other," Herr Hitler stated at another point. "Others are correct when they say: With this world we cannot ever reconcile ourselves."

They fight for the preservation of the gold standard, for example, he added, continuing:

I understand that, for they have the gold. Our gold was plundered and extorted from us.

German productive power is our gold, our capital, and with this gold I can beat any other power in the world.

In opposition to "our social system, where every position will be filled by the most competent son," Herr Hitler asserted, "stands another structure, another world, where the last ideal is always to battle for wealth and for capital, a battle for the egoism of the individual." Furthermore, Hitler said:

The other world says:

If we lose, our capitalistic world building breaks down. Then we have bought gold without purpose. Our entire claim to world domination cannot be maintained if these peoples do away with the money dynasties. They will then come with social demands. A collapse will follow.

And I understand, therefore, when they say: "We want to prevent that under all circumstances."

Those are two worlds. I believe that one of the two worlds must break in pieces. If we collapse the German people will also collapse. If the other world collapses then I am convinced that the world will only then be free.

DIDN'T WANT TO ARM, HE SAYS

Germany did not want to rearm, Herr Hitler told his nationwide audience, because "that devours so much productive power."

"I wanted to employ German productive power for other plans," he said. "I have the ambition to make the German people rich and Germany beautiful. I want the living standard of the individual to be raised. I want us to have the most beautiful and the best culture. I want the theatre and German culture to be for the benefit of the entire people and not only the upper 10,000, as in England.

Those are the stupendous plans for which I needed productive power. Armament only took workers away from me.

Therefore, Herr Hitler declared, he made a proposal that certain armaments be curtailed, that airplanes be removed from war and that bombs be curtailed, out all these proposals, he said, had successively been declined by the other side. These efforts failing, Herr Hitler said, he set himself to the task of rearming with "fanaticism." The result, he added, was that Germany now had so much ammunition that "as the battle came to an end we had employed in all fields hardly a month's ration of our production."

"Today," he went on, "we are armed for every eventuality. England can do what she will. Every week she will receive heavier blows, and if she should set foot anywhere on the continent again then we will introduce ourselves."

There is no power in the world, the Reichsfuehrer asserted, that will be able "against our will" to remove Germans from the territory they now occupy in the West.

As regards aerial warfare Herr Hitler asserted that he had waited three months after the conclusion of the campaign against the French for the British to desist from their "unrestricted air war at night" against the Reich. Not a single armament plant has been forced to shut down as a result of British raids, he added, but "they hit many unhappy families." So, Herr continued:

> I could no longer be responsible before the German people for letting my own national comrades die while sparing strangers. This war has also to be waged, and it is now being waged. It will be waged with determination with the material, with the means and the bravery that are at our disposal.

Germany will determine the hour of decision, Herr Hitler asserted. In such matters, however, he added, he was careful:

"We are so, as a matter of course, convinced of the success of our weapons," the Reichsfuehrer declared, "that we can allow ourselves that. The German people will be able to wait. I believe the German people will be thankful to me when I preferably and frequently wait a bit, with time therewith to spare many sacrifices."

The Reich does not want any "prestige successes," he declared, but allows itself to be led only by military considerations.

"What must happen must happen," Herr Hitler added. "Everything else we want to prevent. In addition, we all have the hope that the hour will one day come in which reason again will be victorious and peace will come."

Throughout his speech Herr Hitler emphasized the conviction that Germany would be victorious. But victory, he declared in his conclusion, will only have been achieved when "a social State has been erected in the Reich" that "must and will be exemplary in all fields of life." The plans and goals that he outlined in his speech, Herr Hitler said, were much easier of achievement "than what lies behind us and will sooner and more surely be arrived at than what until now had to be achieved.

"For the way of a nameless unknown to Fuehrer of the German nation" he declared, "was harder than the way of the Fuehrer of the German nation to that of arbiter of the peace that will come later."

There was no indication in his remarks today how long he expected the war to last. At the same time there was no indication that he expected it to be concluded in the immediate future.

Herr Hitler was greeted upon his arrival at the Borsig plant, after a triumphant automobile ride through the city, by Dr. Robert Ley, head of the German Labor Front; General Field Marshal Wilhelm Keitel, Chief of the Supreme Command of the German Army, and Dr. Fritz Todt, Highways Commissioner. Dr. Joseph Goebbels, Propaganda Minister, introduced Herr Hitler and led the applause at the conclusion of his speech.

Assurances from Hitler

BY THE NEW YORK TIMES | JAN. 2, 1941

HITLER HAS ADDED another promise to the record. This time it is the disavowal of any desire for world conquest. In what is unquestionably a direct reply to President Roosevelt's accusation, the master of the Third Reich declares that to charge Germany with such intentions is to utter "a dumb and infamous lie." Germany, he insists, wants only a just peace and her own place in the sun.

This is plainly an assurance intended to bring aid and comfort to the critics of the President's policy in this country, the advocates of "appeasement" and the opponents of greater aid to Britain. But before these willing listeners put too much faith in it they will do well to remember some of the earlier assurances which have also come from Adolf Hitler, and compare the pledge with the performance. Let us recall a few instances:

The pledge: "After the solution of the Saar question the German Government is willing and determined to accept in its innermost soul the Pact of Locarno." (Jan. 30, 1934.)

The performance: On March 7, 1936, Germany remilitarized the Rhineland in violation of the Locarno treaty.

The pledge: "Germany has neither the wish nor the intention to mix in internal Austrian affairs, or to annex or unite with Austria." (May 21, 1935.)

The performance: On March 12, 1938, Germany annexed Austria.

The pledge: "I repeat here that if this problem [concerning the Sudeten area of Czecho-Slovakia] is solved, there will be no further territorial problems in Europe for Germany…. We do not want any Czechs." (Sept. 26, 1938.)

The performance: On March 14, 1939, Hitler's troops marched into what remained of Czecho-Slovakia and made it German spoils.

The pledge: "We are all determined, and also convinced, that our agreement [with Poland] will bring about lasting and continuous pacification…. We are two peoples. They shall live." (Sept. 26. 1938.)

The performance: At 5:11 on the morning of Sept. 1, 1939, Hitler ordered German troops to attack Poland.

The pledge: "Germany has concluded non-aggression pacts with the Baltic states. Her interests there are exclusively of an economic character." (Oct. 6, 1939.)

The performance: Before dawn on April 9, 1940, German troops marched across Denmark's frontier and German warships attacked Norway.

The pledge: "The new Reich has endeavored to continue the traditional friendship with Holland…. Immediately after I had taken over the government I tried to establish friendly relations with Belgium. … We have given guarantees for the states in the west." (Sept. 26, 1938, and Oct. 6, 1939.)

The performance: Before dawn on the morning of May 10, 1940, the German war machine rode into Belgium and the Netherlands.

The pledge: "We have guaranteed to all contiguous neighbors the inviolability of their territory so far as Germany is concerned. That is not a phrase — that is our sacred will…. Alsace-Lorraine does not exist any more for us…. We want nothing of France, absolutely nothing." (Sept. 26, 1938.)

The performance: On Nov. 30, 1940, the incorporation of Lorraine into the Reich was announced by the German Government. This is a little of the record of the man who now holds out encouragement to the apostles of appeasement in this country and assures them that he has no thought of aggression in any part of the Western Hemisphere, and no dreams of world conquest.

If Napoleon Couldn't, Can Hitler?

BY PHILIP GUEDALLA | FEB. 2, 1941

WHILE ARMIES VEER uncertainly across the map of 1941, it is sobering to turn to the inspection of other armies moving across the map of other years. For we know now precisely where they started from and who led them and how far they got. The causes of their ebb and flow are neatly tabulated in textbooks. Yet, while they were in motion, their impetus and impact were just as incalculable to their contemporaries, as unsolved a riddle, as this morning's news.

When Napoleon jerked himself back onto the throne of France one March day in 1815 and headed north a few weeks later for an easy Anschluss with the Belgians, nobody in London or along the dusty hedgerows before Waterloo had any notion they were living through the Hundred Days and that there were only twelve more days to go; for, "as our ancestors saw it first," the greatest living British historian has written, "they did not know whether the Hundred Days, as we now call them, would not stretch out for a hundred years."

But we know all about them now. The movements are all plain to view in the unwinking light of history. We can discern the causes of that inevitable allied victory won by composite and not wholly satisfactory forces over an incomparable army and predominant gun power, wielded by the greatest soldier of his day. It looked unlikely at the time; it looks unlikely still. But the unanswerable fact remains that it happened.

There is no appeal from the event. It flowed from causes which compelled it. We can analyze them now at leisure. We can see that there was very little need for contemporaries to hold their breath in 1815 since it was the inevitable that happened. If it had not come at Waterloo it would have come on the Rhine or in Lorraine. It might have missed that rainy Sabbath day in June; but in that case it would have come in August or September. We can see it clearly now by the cold light of history; and there is a great deal to be said for steadying our shifting survey of the uncertain present by calm inspection of the fixed unalterable past.

Intelligence is normally employed in arguing from the known to the unknown. What is that we wish to know? It would be satisfactory just now to secure a reasoned forecast of the immediate and ultimate prospects of Adolf Hitler. Well, we know what became of Attila. But examination of the course pursued by barbarian invasions before their inevitable check may well be less instructive than a survey of the victorious aggression of Napoleonic France operating over the fields and cities of a more developed Europe. The parable is less remote. The time is nearer to our own and the conditions of the problem more strictly comparable to those in which the riddle of today presents itself for our solution.

For it is not so long (as history counts time) since another conqueror pitched his armies up and down the map in bold defiance of political geography, improved upon the art of war as practiced by less enterprising adversaries, and sent lines of bayonets marching through the silent streets of subject capitals. We have seen something of the kind in the unpleasant sequence of Warsaw, Oslo, Copenhagen, Amsterdam, Brussels and Paris. But an older Europe saw a similar event unroll itself down a long avenue that ran through even greater cities. For Rome, Vienna, Berlin, Madrid and Moscow is a roll that has a more impressive ring.

But such marches rarely terminate where the commanders call upon the marching lines to halt. The drums still thundered on until tramping feet echoed in the streets of Paris as the allies brought the war home again full-circle to its starting point. For wars have an uncomfortable way of coming home to roost.

Napoleon's was a career of conquest which we may regard according to our point of view as an epic or an outrage. Our judgment of it is irrelevant today. Yet nothing could well be more relevant than a survey of the causes underlying the tremendous ebb and flow of the Napoleonic armies across Europe. What forces sent them forward? Which factors checked them? How many of the same ingredients are present in our own problem? Here are questions worth answering in 1941.

In the first place it is evident that the range of the Napoleonic conquest — compared with the Teutonic raid on Europe — was far wider, both relatively to contemporary means of transport, and even absolutely. Bonaparte's attempt at continental domination opened where Hitler's seems to halt. Late in the Summer weeks of 1805 he switched his striking-force from the hills behind Boulogne to Central Europe. They had been waiting hopefully in full view of the English Channel for the chance to invade England, for the chance that never came. Now, in half an hour of dictation, he launched them at a simpler target — at those Austrians, whom he could always beat. (It is one of Germany's misfortunes that the Austrians and Italians are now there for some one else to beat.) The Austrians were waiting in Bavaria. But Napoleon passed north of them and moved 200,000 men in 16 days into the angle of the Rhine and then wheeled south on a front of 120 miles,

A Soviet propaganda poster published in 1941 reads, "Napoleon was wiped out. Hitler will be wiped out!"

eliminated Mack at Ulm and rode into Vienna. Forty-three days after Ulm the Austrians and the Russians were destroyed at Austerlitz.

Next year the Prussian Army was destroyed at Jena. The Emperor rode into Berlin; and in a campaign of seven weeks he had reduced the Hohenzollerns from a European monarchy to a Baltic principality. That was the tempo of the Napoleonic conquest in an age when armies moved no faster than a marching foot-soldier, and human fancy could not grasp anything more rapid than a man on horseback. For the Emperor had nothing to learn from the Blitzkrieg, so far as his pace was concerned. It was temporarily slowed up by the Winter campaign at the gates of Russia, and even Friedland scarcely served to efface the memory of Eylau.

But Napoleon's range and pace returned in 1808, as he swept into Madrid and out again in menacing pursuit of the British expeditionary force, which the unchanging ubiquity of sea power had planted on the coast of Portugal. The Emperor was soon sweeping across Europe on Vienna. In a five-day manoeuvre he drove the Austrians into Bohemia; and within three weeks of his arrival in Germany he rode into Vienna once again. That Summer there was a good deal of fighting on the level fields outside the city as he tried to convince the Austrians of their defeat at Aspern-Essling they were slow to learn their lesson. But he emphasized the point at Wagram, and one more war wound up in a Napoleonic victory. The hunt was resumed in Eastern Europe, as Napoleon passed 400,000 men in four days across the Niemen into Russia. In 12 weeks he was at Moscow, riding into the last conquered capital of his career. This time a military victory was indecisive, and the geographical achievement of occupying Moscow and thrusting into the heart of Russia proved indecisive too. For the heart of Russia proved to be movable. It was in the Russian armies; and since they managed to elude his blows, Napoleon never reached it with his thrust. (It was the lesson of 1812, and it may well be that of 1940, that a military victory is not necessarily decisive.)

That seemed to be the end. A shrewd English soldier once compared

Napoleon's career to the trajectory of a cannon ball, which must either go on or drop. When he could go on no further, Napoleon dropped; and the stages of his fall are marked by the names of the receding tide of battles fought with decreasing forces as his armies ebbed toward the French frontier. Then the war entered France. Guns thundered at the gates of Paris, and presently the tide of foreign uniforms flowed victoriously through its conquered streets, as a whitefaced man sat huddled in a Russian Army cloak in the far corner of his carriage, while hooting mobs with angry eyes threatened their Emperor on his way to exile. That was the end, until he made a swift return the next year, thrust into Belgium, and tasted final military failure 25 miles from the French frontier at Waterloo.

There in brief panorama is the episode of Napoleon Bonaparte, whose interruption of the course of history ended for himself in tropical exile at St. Helena and for his countrymen in defeat and impaired man power, leading them a generation later to Sedan and, a generation after that, to Vichy.

Is there any parallel with today's phenomenon, the monomaniac who is Europe's lord of misrule from the Russian frontier to the Bay of Biscay? The two men are immeasurably different. As I remember writing in these pages a year or so ago; "Hitler, if his own professions are to be believed, is nothing if not German. This is the authentic warwhoop with which Arminius's braves came yelling through the trees of the Teutoburgerwald at Varus's huddled legionaires. But on which side would you have found Napoleon that day? His place was surely in the Roman ranks. For if ever there was a Latin it was Napoleon Bonaparte."

His clear-cut intelligence, his wine, his women — could anything stand in more vivid contrast with "those solitary reveries on misty mountain tops, that fanaticism about Blood and Breed, that vegetarian celibacy" of the hazy German, intoxicated with false erudition and Wagnerian memories? There is little enough to be learned from a comparison of the two men, since as human beings they are scarcely comparable. But it is not unprofitable to juxtapose their two careers, to confront this morning's newspaper with Napoleon's achievement.

What forces sent Napoleon forward to ephemeral success? Which factors checked him permanently? And how many of them are present in or absent from the challenge of today's German aggression?

His own military genius (and the ineptitude of his adversaries) apart, Napoleon was carried forward to his triumphs on the surge of the French armies. Now the French armies in the first decade of the nineteenth century were moved by a distinctive driving power, which they owed to the French Revolution. It was barely a dozen years since the young republic had faced the world in arms. The challenge of the European monarchies was heard in Paris, where men had dared to execute a king and drown privilege in blood. For the Revolution was not gentle. But to the people who had made it the Revolution stood for their whole future; and when it was challenged, France stood to arms, unfurled the Tricolor and marched to war with beating drums. That was the temper of the French armies after they had made the little general from Corsica First Consul of the Republic, and the First Consul crowned himself Emperor of the French.

For the older men in any unit of the Imperial Army had served in the revolutionary ranks. First called to the colors in the defense of the Revolution, they had marched with Bonaparte into Italy or with Moreau on the Rhine; and the endless wars of the empire were for them a mere continuation of their republican campaigning. They charged at Austerlitz with the same dash, the same contempt for unemancipated enemies as they had experienced in the bright dawn of the republic. The Revolution was a driving power of incomparable force; and the last wash of that tremendous wave still had strength 20 years away to send the Emperor's cuirassiers up the trampled slope toward the British squares at Waterloo.

The motive power of the Revolution was the force by which Napoleon was enabled to drive his imperial juggernaut across Europe. Behind him revolutionary France was a powerhouse. Can we discover any parallel in contemporary Germany? Those eccentrics who can still detect any traces of genuine revolutionary impulse in the sordid alternation of trickery and violence by which Nazi showmanship imposed itself upon the German Republic may proclaim that here once more a revolution faces the world in arms.

Was it a revolution? Are we really sure that the same human impulses which stormed the Bastille burned the Reichstag? Is the Horst Wessel song a "Marseillaise"? And were the Nazi nominees of Rhenish heavy industry the young Dantons of a new republic? The French of '93 were fighting to be free. The Germans of today are fighting to be conquerors. They announce it once a week to conquered Poles and Dutchmen. Tribal impulse or a nation's lust for international revenge may be a formidable thing. But it bears no possible resemblance to the swinging step that carries men forward to their freedom. That was the pace at which the French armies hurried across Europe. That force sustained them; and it was eventually canalized to turn the grinding mills of the Napoleonic Empire.

But there is nothing of the kind discernible in Germany today. Pride wounded by military failure to snatch world victory in 1918; a craving for revenge; unpleasant outcrops of old tribal savagery; pride of race—these are the dark ingredients of the Nazi brew. Skillful distillery may render them intoxicating for a time to limited sections of a dosed population. But that drugged onset of a hypnotized community has nothing in common with the charging step that sent the Tricolor and the "Marseillaise" half way round the world a century ago.

There is no analogy between the revolutionary era and our own. If there is any parallel with ours it lies in the Elizabethan age — that "dangerous world of ideologies, despots, persecutions, treacherous propaganda and broken treaties, of war under the pretense of peace." That was a time when England once again was the last fortress of the world's freedom and English eyes were strained into the Channel mists for the first sight of the Armada. But the French Empire breathed another air — the atmosphere of easy growth that follows the great rains of true revolution.

There is another difference besides. A French invasion under Napoleon was a formidable thing. But it carried with it certain advantages for those classes of society which were the beneficiaries of the French Revolution. Old privileges vanished in a revolutionary blaze of tricolors. Dynasties seemed to evaporate; law was largely simplified; philosophy appeared to gain what organized religion sometimes lost. For, strangely enough, a European was sometimes freer under French administration than he had been in the shadow of his native feudalism. The foreign conqueror positively threatened to deprive Spain of the Inquisition.

But what man is freer where the German treads today? Ask them in Amsterdam and Oslo and Paris. The Nazi brings his own inquisition in the shuttered automobiles of the Gestapo. No foreign population can delude itself with hopes of enlarged freedom as the swastika flutters up to its masthead. There are no foreign units in the German Army; yet Napoleon's forces were full of foreign elements. Polish lancers, Italian troopers rode with his veterans. But Norwegian infantry is rarely seen in German columns. No Poles, no Dutchmen and no Czechs march with their conquerors. Each conquest has only served to add another weight to the growing burden of world dominion, to stretch the straining cord of power a little tighter.

Is there any parallel between the Napoleonic age and ours? Then, as now, a growing circle of threatened peoples faced the challenge of a conqueror. But then he was sustained by the forces inherent in revolution and denied to servile Germany today. Those forces drove the engine of his power and prolonged his term of conquest.

There have been other efforts by other individuals at single-handed domination of the world. From time to time a Roman Emperor achieved it by reason of the simple fact that he had gained control of the Roman administrative and military machine and of the vast area already subject to it. Other barbarian raiders from the East — Attila, Tamerlane, Genghis Khan — leaped into the saddle of world dominion with a running start, barbarism impinging suddenly on the settled civilizations.

Is that the true analogy with all we are facing now? It may be. Hitler's epiphany has far more in common with the racing hordes of high-cheeked savages that broke in spray across the world than with the steady tramp of the Old Guard, the pounding charge of his cuirassiers rising in their stirrups with a roar of "Vive l'Empereur!" as they swept past the small, great-coated figure on the gray barb. For he was an eagle among conquerors. But now we face a vulture.

PHILIP GUEDALLA IS AN ENGLISH HISTORIAN AND BIOGRAPHER.

Rogue's Progress: 1933–1942

BY THE NEW YORK TIMES | JAN. 30, 1942

NINE YEARS AGO today Adolf Hitler became Chancellor of Germany. He beaded a coalition government of National Socialists and Nationalists. In the presence of the aged and failing President von Hindenburg he took a solemn oath of allegiance to the Constitution of the German Republic, which he then proceeded to destroy. It is fitting that we should commemorate this anniversary. There is no better way of recalling the nine years of history than by quoting from Hitler's own statements made each year on or near the date of Jan. 30. Here are some of his own words:

1933 — The Marxist parties and their lackeys have had fourteen years to show what they can do. The result is a heap of ruins. Now, people of Germany, give us four years and then pass judgment upon us.

1934 — Without wishing to meddle in the slightest degree in the internal affairs of other nations …

1935 — [To the people of the Saar, after the plebiscite.] After your return, the German Reich has no more territorial demands on France.

1933 — Germany does not wish to attack these [new European] states. Above all, Poland will remain Poland.

1937 — The German Government has assured Belgium and Holland of its readiness to recognize and guarantee these states as untouchable and neutral regions for all time.

1938 — The German people is no war-like nation.

1939 — Germany wishes to live in peace and on friendly terms with all nations, including America.

1940 — They wanted war. They shall have it.

1941 — I am convinced that 1941 will be the crucial year of the great new order in Europe.

These excerpts are of necessity incomplete. Other, and equally illuminating passages, can be found. No doubt the Hitlerian philosophy will be again expounded today, in Hitler's inimitable manner. It is not likely that he will promise his people victory in 1942. Presumably he will be obliged to suggest that it will be 1943 before three-fourths of the population, of the globe, now outside his system, will kneel in chains at his command. His reputation as regards honor, consistency and veracity will remain what it is today. Nothing can shake it.

He should have an anniversary message from the American people. We believe it could fittingly be in his own words of 1940, with a change of pronoun. We think the American people and their friends can now see far enough ahead to say to him: "You wanted war. You shall have it."

Again Hitler Rewrites Vital Page of History

BY EDWIN L. JAMES | **FEB. 1, 1942**

WHEN ADOLF HITLER sets out to write — or rewrite — history he does what must be a job satisfactory to himself for he never has any difficulty in proving his points from the record as he concocts it. But his versions will scarcely satisfy any one who cares anything about the truth of the record.

In his speech Friday in Berlin the Fuehrer rewrote a couple of pages of history in a manner that would be comic were not the author the father of the present war in which the lives and happiness of so many millions are at stake.

Hitler turned to the subject of the second World War. He set out to prove the similarity between the first and second World Wars. In the first place, Germany was to blame for neither.

Both wars, he said, were forced upon Germany. The Fuehrer did not carry the parallel far enough to mention that it was Germany which invaded Belgium in 1914 and Germany which invaded Belgium in 1940.

It was the same power, England, he declared, which started both wars. But he had something new on the Kaiser. Wilhelm never blamed the Jews for his troubles, whereas Hitler finds that both World Wars were really started by the Jews.

Then there was Churchill, "the warmonger" in both wars. That was a good British link. Then his imagination fixed on Roosevelt and he finds that Roosevelt was the right-hand man of Woodrow Wilson, whom he designates as that "arch-liar." So there it is — plain and simple. Churchill and Roosevelt had much to do with the first World War and the same men are responsible for the second World War.

AS FOR MR. ROOSEVELT

The record shows that Franklin D. Roosevelt was assistant secretary of the Navy during the participation of the United States in the first World War. The record indicates he was pretty good at that job. But the idea that he was the right-hand man of President Wilson is unique in its novelty. True, such a statement fits in with Hitler's argument, but it does not fit in with the facts. One wonders if Hitler ever heard of Colonel House.

But the craziest of Hitler's statements Friday was the following:

> Before the first World War England was a little island with relatively no importance; Germany was a grand colonial power.

Well, Hitler said the first World War started in 1914; he had that right. In 1914 the British Empire was a pretty sizable undertaking. Canada, Australia, New Zealand, India, South Africa and the rest were then members of the British Empire.

Nor was Germany a great colonial empire. She had the Pacific islands which her ally, Japan, now has, and she had three colonies in Africa, with which she never did anything worthwhile and which were always a drain.

"SOME LITTLE ISLAND"

Of course, Hitler was trying to show that the "little island" of 1914 became the great British Empire by what it got from Germany. To paraphrase Mr. Churchill — "some little island." Hitler did not explain in detail how England, which in 1914 was a little island, got enough land from Germany now to rule one-fourth of the world. And that one-fourth was wrong; it is one-sixth.

Naturally, Hitler dug up the old fable that Germany was not beaten in 1918, but was fooled by Wilson's Fourteen Points. He gives an extra sting by saying the German people "did not know they were dealing with a paralytic and an idiot."

This old story that Germany was not beaten in 1918 is rather stale; no serious student of the situation has ever felt that Germany would have touched Wilson's Fourteen Points with a 20-foot pole had she not been looking for a way to escape a disastrous debacle.

When Hitler started out his mentor and friend was General Ludendorff. When the first World War ended Ludendorff was quartermaster general of the German Army and Hitler was a corporal. It is fair enough to assume that the general had a rather broader and better view of the situation than the corporal.

It is, therefore, not without interest to turn to Vol. II of the memoirs of Ludendorff, published under the title of "Ludendorff's Own Story." In the latter part of this volume he reviews the position of the German armies and the situation at home and, as he wrote on Page 372:

> In these circumstances I felt compelled to undertake the responsible task of hastening the end of the war.

That was written as of Sept. 9. Ludendorff and the other German leaders then debated for two weeks whether to try the path of Wilson's Fourteen Points or to ask the Queen of Holland to intervene with a request for an armistice. Ludendorff tells of the fateful meeting with the Kaiser at Spa in the last days of September, when it was decided that in view of the bad military position and difficult conditions at home Wilson should be asked to arrange an armistice.

AND GERMANY CAPITULATED

So much has been made of the argument that German leaders blindly accepted promises they thought Wilson had made and that they were, therefore, victims, that it is worthwhile to read from Page 418 of Ludendorff's Vol. II:

> On Oct. 23 or 24 Wilson's answer arrived. It was a strong answer to our cowardly note. This time he made it quite clear that the armistice conditions must be such as to make it impossible for Germany to resume hostilities and to give the powers allied against her unlimited power to settle themselves the details of the peace accepted by Germany.

And then on Page 425:

> In the German note of Oct. 27 we capitulated.

So General Ludendorff thought Germany was defeated. And Corporal Hitler thought Germany was swindled.

As the Fuehrer puts it now:

> *There came an armistice which meant the total destruction of Germany and the peace treaty which followed completed the looting of Germany and the deprivation of all her rights, through an international financial plot.*

HE LOOKS TO FUTURE

After explaining that the present war, too, was a plot against the Third Reich, Hitler explained that when the cold weather is over he will smash back the Russian Army again. He explained that Roosevelt was a "fool" and a "stooge" for Churchill and expressed the idea that his U-boats would show the United States what they could do. He did not say Germany would win the war in 1942, but he said it would be a year of great victories. In Russia, he said, "Our day will come again."

He ended:

> *This is the prayer that will be heard: O God, give us the strength to obtain liberty for our people, for our children and for our grandchildren and not only for the German people but for all the peoples of Europe, for this is a war for all Europe and therefore for the whole of humanity.*

That almost recalls the Kaiserliche "Gott mit Uns."

The next time Hitler undertakes to unscramble history, he might take a shot at explaining this passage from a speech he made at Danzig on Sept. 19, 1939:

> *Now, gentlemen of the great British Empire, the aims of Germany are closely limited. We discussed the matter with Russia — they, after all, are the most immediately interested neighbors and if you are of the opinion that we might come to a conflict on the subject — we will not.*

CHAPTER 5

Hitler's Decline

By 1942, the startling German advance across Europe
and North Africa had come to a halt. Furthermore, the
Japanese attack on Pearl Harbor in Dec. 1941 had brought
the United States into the war, and Germany now faced a
powerful enemy whose home territory had not been rav-
aged by war. The Germans faced a difficult path to victory,
but the Fuehrer remained fervent in tone and consistent
in his message. Under his command, the Germans would
fight — to the death, if it came to that. At home, Hitler's
popularity declined.

Hitler's Real 'Kampf'

BY WALTER BROWN | **JUNE 14, 1942**

This Summer promises to bring the big crisis in the career of the Fuehrer. His
enemies are closing in on him. From what is known of his character, his future
course may be conjectured.

IN THIS FATEFUL SUMMER of 1942 Adolf Hitler faces the greatest crisis of
his turbulent career. No other moment in his lifetime — he has recently
turned 53 — has seen the chance for sweeping victory so finely balanced
with the possibility of doom. Before him he has a Russia which has
proved its powers of resistance in a year of fearful war; ahead, too, is the
rising might of the United Nations and the slow-festering hatred of all
the millions on the conquered continent. Victory now could seal his conquests for decades; defeat would send him and his nation to destruction.

What manner of man is Adolf Hitler? In his outward appearance
the Fuehrer shows few of the attributes of greatness; dressed in civil-

ian clothes and in with a crowd he would not stand out might easily pass unrecognized. Much of his bearing as the Fuehrer of the Reich depends on his uniform and the appurtenances of power which surround him. He shows few signs of his advancing age; he still has a full head of hair, with only slight traces of gray visible at the temples. His famous forelock, which, with his mustache, was formerly his outstanding characteristic, today is brushed back and falls forward in the old familiar way only in the heat of oratory or emotion. When it does, he sweeps it back with a quick, nervous gesture which has become typical; at times, when speaking, he combs his fingers through it in an exhausted fashion after a particularly emphatic passage.

His hair is always carefully trimmed, close-shaven at the nape of the neck. Small details such as this, observed when one is close to him, are evidence of the meticulous care he expends on his appearance. His mustache has grown fuller with the years, giving him a more dignified expression. His fingernails are always manicured, his hands are white and expressive; they are not the hands of a laborer. He has a personal barber who sees to these details.

Of late Hitler has shown an inclination to stoutness. Though far from fat, he has filled out noticeably, and when he wears the brown shirt of the Storm Troops he shows a paunch. His face is no longer thin and has lost much of its former fanatic expression. At close range it has an unhealthy, yellowish look; the skin is flabby and somewhat oily. His eyes are deep-set, with dark pouches beneath them. His nose is firm and rather pointed, the strongest feature of his face. His chin is weak, his mouth small, with thin, rather colorless lips which he frequently purses in a frown. His face has a wide range of expression; at times it can be very cruel; at other times, notably when he speaks to small children, it relaxes to gentleness and kindness. He has a great fondness for children, and they appear to trust him instinctively, laughing and playing freely in his presence.

In his private life the Fuehrer shows a taste for grandeur which smacks of the nouveau riche. He lives in Berlin and Berchtesgaden, in surroundings of ostentatious, often almost morbid, splendor. He took pride in planning the Long Hall of the new Chancellery in Berlin to be longer than the Hall of Mirrors at Versailles, and similar lavish tastes in architecture and decoration are evident in other rooms of the Chancellery and in the Berghof, his private home above Berchtesgaden.

But when he is at the front — which is almost constantly while a campaign is in progress — Hitler lives in traditional Spartan fashion. Besides his field headquarters he maintains also a complete mobile headquarters set up in a special train. This likewise is equipped with every facility for keeping in touch with operations at the front; complete radio, field telephone and telegraph equipment, a staff of clerks and stenographers, teletype machines and the like. Hitler is said to work his staff hard, and he himself requires but little rest, often getting along on four or five hours' sleep for prolonged periods.

His greatest asset in his approach to military problems is said to be a simplicity of thought, the direct logic of a mind untrammeled by traditional military training. He plunges to the heart of the problem, mapping his solutions in broad outline. In the Reichschancellery, when he began his intensive studies, Hitler had set up a huge sandbox on which tactical problems were represented and then worked out in minute detail. He developed an admiration for the teachings of von Clausewitz, which could, he was said to maintain, only today be fully developed through the resources of modern armies. His campaigns during actual warfare are worked out in much the same fashion, in conferences with his staff, who fill in the details of the outline he presents.

Psychologically, Hitler presents a confusing and complex problem. A thousand solutions have been offered to the riddle of this man. As he could never understand the world around him, or bring himself in harmony with other human beings, so could the world not comprehend him.

In the loneliness of his life there is one key to his character. Since his earliest childhood Hitler has had no intimate confidant. The only person, so he has said, who really understood him was his mother; she died when he was still a boy. He played no games, took no part in the normal comradeship of boyhood, but lived in a world of his own, his mind occupied with dreams, with adult problems, with bitterness at his lowly station. Later, when he was forced to work as a laborer, he likewise found no contact with his fellows. They thought him surly; he became enraged at their failure to follow his sweeping ideas, at their acceptance of their lot. He formed, then, a contempt for the masses which he never lost.

In war he found the greatest contentment of his early years. He had, and has today, no lack of courage. But it is courage of the exalted kind which does not realize danger, an almost servile submission to the spiritual uplift experienced in completing a high mission for superiors. It is not the stubborn courage born of deep-rooted convictions. It is said of the Fuehrer that once he descends from his exalted state and senses the possibility of failure he can become almost craven.

Hitler is, without doubt, an intuitive type. Seeing things only in broadest outline, he is unhampered by the fear of difficulties inherent in details. He is quick to seize on obvious weaknesses of his opponents, impatient with those who point out their strength. His intuition works offensively, driving him ahead.

Hitler's hysterical rages are common knowledge, but whether he is a victim of true hysteria is a question which has still not been satisfactorily answered. Germans once close to him believe that he deliberately exaggerates his rage to force others to his point of view.

The most vital question facing the world today is: How would Hitler react to a real setback? How has his thinking and planning been affected by his initial failure to conquer the Russians? Hitherto the Fuehrer has been able to remain always one stride ahead of the world, never relinquishing the "law of action?" Now, finally, the world is catching up with him. What will, he do under these circumstances?

The question is difficult, but the answer may come more quickly than has appeared possible. Broad planning reaches its limits, and there comes a time when details demand attention. That may be the turning point for a man of Hitler's character, the moment when hysteria becomes real. Faced by the unconquerable logic of force, intuition may fail. Difficulties hitherto ignored become suddenly real, plans are upset, the whole structure of long-range strategy totters. If calm reason cannot be brought into play, catastrophe may well be imminent.

Hitler was warned against the Russian venture. Many of his generals were against it, as were his closest party comrades, Hess and Goering. The former is known to have foreseen disaster, so much so that he was willing to risk the ultimate to avoid it Goering is reported to have warned Hitler that Germany had not the planes for a major air war on several fronts.

Thus far it seems that Hitler miscalculated. He had sized up the democracies correctly, but he failed to see in communism the very revolutionary strength that was Nazi Germany's. His strategy failed. In the face of mounting difficulties he became impatient with his generals and once more relied on his intuition. But he could not resume the offensive.

Today Hitler's chief commanders are at the front once more. It may well prove that they, not the Fuehrer, will henceforth have the decisive voice in future operations in Russia. Hitler, on the defensive, with no scope for intuitive planning, becomes commonplace and wavering in his ideas. He may have another great plan, but the limitations of conquest now hamper him. He may strike, but it will not be with the old power. What seems most probable is that he will let others be the guiding voice in his planning.

Hitler Said to Lose Little Man's Faith

BY GEORGE AXELSSON | DEC. 3, 1942

STOCKHOLM, SWEDEN, DEC. 2 — The little man in Germany has now lost all faith in Adolf Hitler, according to Berlin reports from qualified observers, received here through private channels.

"Instead of worrying about the soldiers out on the Russian snows the Fuehrer spends his days in luxury and safety in his Berchtesgaden mountain palace devoting hours at a time in solitary trance before the picture of Mona Lisa which he has stolen from France" is one of the many things persons say more or less openly in Berlin, if the reports are to be believed.

Throughout the Autumn Berlin has lived in fear of the American Flying Fortresses. The fact that these have not yet appeared has done nothing to abate the fear, for Berliners still think they may come any night.

Invalid soldiers are seen on almost all Berlin streets. Young blind soldiers with yellow armbands grope about. There also are legless and armless veterans.

Many drunken persons are seen on Berlin streets, indicating Germans are making liquor at home because of the shortage in the open market. Liquor from home stills is making the Germans boisterous or quarrelsome and in the hangover stage more ill-humored.

Indicating that the Germans are bad losers and cannot take reverses, discourtesy and ill-humor are more common. The effect of the Goebbels courtesy campaign in the early part of the year was short-lived.

Gloom is the order of the day in the capital. The authorities are doing what they can to raise morale. For Christmas extra rations of flour, butter and coffee have been allowed. To brighten up the streets after dark shops need not black out their windows until 7 P. M. this month. A similar measure was taken last December.

Last December some small Christmas things could still be bought in the stores. This year it is impossible to buy even a pad of writing paper. The stores do not even honor official buying permits, against which last year one could insist on getting such items as hats, gloves and socks.

The Berliner who eats out is looking forward to a dreary holiday because restaurants and other amusement places are out of liquors and wines. The only way to get a bottle of even new Rhine wine in a restaurant these days is to pass the waiter a bag of coffee under the table.

The Ascent and Decline of Adolf Hitler

BY ANNE O'HARE MCCORMICK | JAN. 30, 1943

HISTORY is likely to show that the rise and fall of Adolf Hitler as a world figure was encompassed within a decade. On the tenth anniversary of his accession to power in Germany he is far from being finished, and it is too trivial an interpretation of the tragedy of our time to imagine that it is due to one man alone, or to the ambition, the blindness or the complaisance of the leaders who shared the stage with Hitler as the drama developed.

Nevertheless he is the fateful figure of this fateful decade. As in Germany he rose to the surface by stirring up assorted hates, frustrations and primitive cruelties to use as currency for his own intrigues for power, so in the world he became the rallying point for thwarted ambitions and forces of destruction which he employed in much the same manner as instruments for his own plans for conquest. He is at once the symptom of the sickness of a nation and the carrier by which that sickness was borne across frontiers to prey on the weakness and weariness of other nations.

He is not yet defeated, but as the Hitlerian decade ends the doom that has pursued him from the beginning has caught up with him. He was always, a figure of doom. One saw it back in 1933, when the first surprise at his own success had not worn off and when, in the course of a single interview, he gravitated between the extremes of bombastic self-assurance and almost pathetic uncertainty and doubt.

He appeared then as a man driven by inner furies, pulled in two directions at once, and no one who has watched him in the years since, particularly in his great moments — in the Rhineland following the remilitarization, receiving Sir John Simon and Anthony Eden after he had declared conscription, reviewing his troops as they marched into Vienna, at the head of his generals on the eve of the second great "blitz" — could escape the impression that the trail of tragedy that followed his triumphs enveloped him too, a kind of physical aura.

He was always alone in the crowds, walking in a self-created vacuum, and yet he could never bear to be alone, because he was haunted by premonitions, fears of disaster and fears of death. He was never satisfied, because there was always something lacking in his successes.

The best military observers in Berlin used to say that he was a commander of strictly limited objectives and would not go farther than he could with safety. It was this conception that let him go too far. Nor did it take into account that Hitler's mind, like his appetite, had no boundaries. He was the first of contemporary leaders to think "globally," but in his case it was not because he knew the world was small.

He knew nothing of the world beyond the borders of the Reich and the exciting picture books of Haushofer. It was because he saw himself so large that the earth looked like the estate of Adolf Hitler.

But the truth that neither the outside world nor the great part of Germany itself could credit was that Hitler was in love with war. In a new biography by Ludwig Wagner called "Hitler, Man of Strife," it is related that a few days after he became Chancellor he sent out two clerks to a large bookshop in the Potsdammerplatz to purchase all available books on Napoleon.

Yet Napoleon was not Hitler's hero. In that first interview he told this reporter that the historical figure he most admired was not the Corsican, not Frederick the Great and certainly not Bismarck. It was Oliver Cromwell, he insisted, and though in 1933 this was explainable on the ground that he was thinking primarily in terms of the conquest of the Reich, he repeated the statement long after he had broken the bounds and started on the career of aggression. But as soon as he arrived in a place of power, he wanted to study the career of Napoleon.

He was already determined to overshadow Napoleon and succeed where the other Little Corporal failed. He was talking peace, but every move he made from 1933 to 1939 was in preparation for war. To an observer who saw him last in 1940 it was at once evident that he was more at ease, firmer and fitter, in military uniform than he had ever been in his brown tunic. He seemed to have found himself and shed his unease and his frustrations in the great business of war. And this was natural; one saw in a flash that of course war was his business. His genius is the genius of destruction. He had forged all his grievances against society, all the sickness of his soul, all the hates he had churned up in the dregs of the German spirit, into bombers and machine guns and armored divisions.

The decade of his power is over — and while he has not yet been stopped, either by Russia or by Britain and the United States, he is already defeated by the one power he has conquered, the one power he willed to conquer. All Hitler really wanted, as he told us in "Mein Kampf," was the domination of Europe. He was indifferent to colonies in Africa or Asia. Europe was the colony he coveted. And if he had been able to possess Europe, either by force or persuasion, if Europe had accepted the New Order under Germany, the outer world could have battled the walls of the fortress in vain. But Europe has rejected him, and it is Europe, above all, that disrupted captive and "dying" continent, which proves that he is doomed.

Hitler's Biggest Lie

BY EDWIN L. JAMES | APRIL 11, 1943

Therewith one started out with the very correct assumption that in the size of the lie there is always contained a certain factor of credibility, since the great masses of a people may be more corrupt in the bottom of their hearts than they will be consciously and intentionally bad, therefore with the primitive simplicity of their minds they will more easily fall victims to a great lie than to a small one. — "Mein Kampf"

IT IS QUITE EVIDENT that when one undertakes to pick the biggest lie told by Adolf Hitler one at once undertakes to cover a wide territory indeed. The very record of the man is marked by a series of falsifications and deceptions perhaps beyond the record of any other man who has played a role in public life.

The record is too long and fulsome to make practicable anything like a complete analysis. One might, in a short symposium, start out with the statement by Hitler in a speech in Berlin on Feb. 10, 1933, in which he said: "The first and best point of the government's program is that we won't lie and we won't swindle." One might dig up the Fuehrer's promise to Prime Minister Chamberlain that if he got the Sudetenland he would have fulfilled all of his territorial ambitions in Europe. One might refer to his declaration on Nov. 10, 1933: "I am not so senseless as to want war. We want peace and understanding, nothing else." Or one might turn to this effusion on Jan. 13, 1934: "We do not wish to interfere with the rights of others, to restrict the lives of other peoples, to oppress or subjugate other peoples."

Or one might also turn to his declaration before the Reichstag on March 7, 1936: "We have no territorial demands to make in Europe?' Or how about his proclamation on Jan. 30, 1937: "The German Government has assured Belgium and Holland of its readiness to recognize and guarantee those States as untouchable and neutral regions for all times."

One might recall his declaration on Sept. 16, 1938: "We want nothing from France — nothing at all." Or on April 28, 1939, his statement: "The Czech nation deserves our respect." And on Sept. 1, 1939, he said: "I will not war against women and children. I have ordered our air force to restrict itself to attacks on military objectives." And how about this one on Dec. 10, 1940: "We have demanded nothing of others. We have been drawn into a war against our will"?

The story can be dragged out. There is his statement on Jan. 30, 1941: "When I came to power I did not wish to carry out my program by force. Instead I did my utmost to accomplish my purpose by persuasion alone." But after going over the entire sorry record one comes to the conclusion that in its import internationally, in its reflection on the world situation, the biggest lie Hitler has told is his story that Germany was not defeated in 1918.

When we look at the war today and when we look forward to the possibility of a German effort to stage a defeat again, our attention must turn to the tale that Germany was not beaten militarily at the end of the last war but that an unconquered Germany was duped by an American President into laying down her arms in the expectation of not having to pay for losing a war which the Kaiser had started in 1914.

Interestingly enough, Hitler espoused this lie only late in his program of falsification. In "Mein Kampf" he nowhere argued that Germany was swindled by Wilson in 1918. On the contrary, he took the position that if Germany was defeated in 1918, Germany deserved her defeat. He blamed it on the processes of democracy, on the press, on the Jews. But he did not blame it on Wilson.

On page 309 of the Reynal & Hitchcock edition of "Mein Kampf" Hitler wrote:

Unfortunately, the military defeat of the German people is not an undeserved catastrophe but rather a deserved punishment by eternal retribution. We more than deserved this defeat.

It is worthwhile noting that although Hitler in "Mein Kampf" did not make use of the argument that Germany had been cheated in 1918, that thesis had been popular in certain quarters in Germany for years before "Mein Kampf" was completed.

The Fuehrer had mentioned the idea several times in his speeches, and when he handed the armistice terms to the French in 1940 he trotted out the theory that Germany had really not been defeated in a war which had" been forced upon her in 1914. On the contrary, it was his story that the Reich had been outrageously short-changed.

It is well to quote the German statement handed to the French on June 21, 1940:

In reliance on assurances given to the German Reich by the American President Wilson and confirmed by the Allied Powers, German armed forces laid down their arms in November, 1918.

Therewith was ended a war which the German people and its government had not wanted and in which the enemy, despite enormous superiority, did not successfully in any way conquer the German Army, Navy or German Air Force.

However, at the moment of the arrival of the German Armistice Commission, violation of the ceremoniously given promises began. On Nov. 11, 1918, in this car began the time of suffering of the German people.

What dishonor and humiliation, what human and material suffering could be caused had its outlet here. Broken promises and perjury conspired against a people which after more than four years of heroic resistance had only one weakness — belief in the promises of democratic statesmen.

That was the first time Hitler had used this lie with full dramatic effect. But it was a beginning. After having cooked up the case by degrees be launched forward on a well-staged presentation of this idea in his New Year's message to the German people. Yet it is to he noted that even then he did not depart entirely from his preachments in "Mein Kampf." Here is a characteristic passage from his speech:

When the German people, weakened at home by revolution, later laid down their arms, simple-minded people, relying on the promises of these faithless enemies, thought they could expect a peace based on justice, reconciliation and good-will.

From that day onward the name of the President of the United States is connected for all time with the biggest fraud in world history which followed. By undermining the morale of the German people, unconquered on the field of battle, he made possible its destruction.

At the same time Wilson has forever rendered the German nation immune against the repetition of any such attempt. From that time onward the word of an American President counts for no more, at any rate to the German people, than in the United States: that is to say, precisely nothing.

When it came to the tenth anniversary of the Nazi accession to power Hitler had read for him a statement to the German people. He came back to the idea that an undefeated Germany had been swindled in 1918. Again he mixed his idea of the blame falling on German revolutionists and on President Wilson. This is how he put it:

After a heroic resistance which could not be broken by any enemy throughout four years of struggle defeatist elements, both from within and without, forced her [Germany] into open revolution.

The American President Wilson with his Fourteen Points conjured up a vision of future peace which was eagerly seized upon by the German people — more so as there had been no positive war aims either among the great masses or among leading personalities.

The nation was fighting for its mere existence and some sections of the population was therefore almost grateful to have a peace of conciliation and understanding offered it.

Immediately after the German people had thus been induced to give up their arms there came a historic swindle, a breach of promise such as world history had never known before. Instead of a peace of good-will and understanding came the Diktat of Versailles, which debased the German nation and the nations allied to her to the level of slaves, made them militarily defenseless, deprived them of their political rights and in the economic sphere destroyed them for an incalculable period.

Now there we have a picture. It is Hitler's claim that Germany was not defeated in 1918, that she was deceived into laying down her arms and that after she had taken that step she was tricked and cheated. That is Hitler's story, his biggest lie.

It is naturally interesting to speculate on why Hitler took up the story of Germany's not having been defeated in 1918. He espoused it only in 1935, 10 years after "Mein Kampf" had been written and more than two years after he had come to power. It had been available for a decade, but there is lacking any evidence that he made it his own in those years.

One may argue that by 1935 he had decided upon a new European war and that the argument that Germany had been imposed upon was good for that purpose. There is much to be said for that theory, but a study of the man would indicate that, after some hesitation, he had fixed upon the tale because it fitted into his bombastic psychology. Why it did not appeal to him earlier is a question that is not easy to answer. But, once he had adopted it as his own, he made the most of it. He has not been prominent recently in public appearances, but in such as have evolved and in his statements read by lieutenants he has tried to make the most of a bathetic falsehood.

And now again a Germany at war is not having such a happy time. There are here and there reports of German peace feelers and many rumors that Germany may soon try again to stage a defeat in a manner to avoid the appearance of having been bested on the field of battle.

What is there, if anything, to Hitler's story of 1918? Most people in the world were of the opinion that if Germany had not been facing defeat in 1918 it would not have made any difference whether Wilson in January of 1918 had put forward 14 or 1,400 points — the Germans would have paid not the slightest attention to him. Had they not shown in the Treaty of Brest-Litovsk what sort of peace they would make when they could? Was there any good-will and understanding in that document? Also there was not lacking evidence of the peace they would have made with Britain, France and the United States had they been able to put it over. There was no brotherly love there.

So what is there to the Hitler tale?

Fortunately there exists on the record material for an answer to the Fuehrer. In 1918 he was an infantry corporal. In the Spring of 1918 he had a dose of the poison gas, the use of which his countrymen initiated in 1915, and he had to have long treatment to regain his sight. He probably did not know himself much about what was going on in the conduct of the war.

But there is another man who was in a better position to know. He was General Erich Ludendorff, Quartermaster General of the German Army and through the fighting of 1918 second in command to Field Marshal Paul von Hindenburg. Strangely enough, in the Putsch of 1923 which landed Hitler in prison, Ludendorff was his associate in the Brown Shirt movement. But what is more important was that Ludendorff has put down in writing his story of the last years of the war. It is intriguing, therefore, to use the material of Ludendorff, the Quartermaster General, or Chief of Staff, in 1918 to prove that Hitler, the infantry corporal, did not know what went on.

Ludendorff's story shows that as far back as November, 1916, there was much doubt among the army leaders that Germany could win the war and then, almost two years before the war ended, there was no little discussion of peace possibilities.

Ludendorff recorded a message written to Kaiser Wilhelm on June 27, 1917, in which von Hindenburg said:

"Our greatest anxiety at this moment, however, is the decline in the national spirit. It must be revived or we shall lose the war."

The Quartermaster General devoted pages to development in the Summer of 1917 when he foresaw grave difficulties because of the discouragement of the German people. One of his remarks was "The Lord in Heaven forsook His German nation because it had forsaken itself." He told of the hopes he put in the Pope's peace proposals in August and of his disappointment when the Allied Nations did not respond favorably. He told of efforts to send out peace feelers in September and again in October, but the French were wary. Here is a paragraph from page 134 of Vol. XI:

> *I also entertained some hopes of the efforts being made by the representatives of the Foreign Office in Brussels, Herr von der Lancken, who sought to get in touch with French statesmen. He went to Switzerland, but the gentlemen from France stayed away.*

Ludendorff showed bitterness because the collapse of Russia had not been followed by a reestablishment of German morale. He complained that the German prisoners released by Russia seemed to have been inoculated by considerable Bolshevik propaganda, and at one point he even expressed doubts that Germany had acted wisely in sending Lenin from Switzerland to Russia.

Ludendorff reached the beginning of 1918 convinced that Germany could not get a "just" peace. He found that the Allies would not quit on the basis of the status quo ante. And thus he prepared the German 1918 offensives.

After the success of the German Spring drive Ludendorff was rather astonished that the Allies showed no wish to quit. He found France wobbly and England in trouble. Then, for the first time he spoke of the coming American divisions.

Recording that the unrestricted submarine war was not bringing the results the Kaiser had hoped for, he wrote: "From our previous experiences with the submarine warfare, I expected strong forces of Americans to come. But the rapidity with which they actually did arrive proved surprising."

Ludendorff then threw himself into the plan for the second German offensive of May, 1918. He did not show great hopes for large results.

"I had many conversations," he wrote, "with officers of all ranks and they all complained of the tired and discontented spirit which was being brought into the army from home.... I repeatedly spoke with the

Erich Ludendorff, German quartermaster general during World War I and participant in the Beer Hall Putsch of 1923.

authorities concerned about the spirit of the people at home. In those days I was for the first time met with the reply that men were also returning from the army discontented and tired of war."

As Ludendorff recorded, the Germans had no small military success in June. But he added: "It was certainly discouraging that our two great attacks had not forced a decision. That they had been victories was obvious. Disillusionment had come. It was impossible in this World War to gloss that over. The reason for the falling off in our morale was not to be found in that. It lay very much deeper."

Much attention was given by the Quartermaster General to the failing of discipline in the army. He had hundreds of complaints against officers, and soldiers actually protested that the officers had better quarters and better food than they. He found all this unreasonable and traitorous; yet, he concluded, it was a factor that had to be reckoned with. Allied propaganda, he found, was too effective and the German response ineffectual.

Ludendorff then told of peace talks in June but had to record that they came to nothing. "In view of Clemenceau's speeches," he wrote, "We were compelled to continue the war or submit to humiliation." And he added: "England and the United States wished for our economic destruction. England, in addition, wanted to render us powerless and France to bleed us white. Common to all our antagonists was the desire to inflict the deepest humiliation on their hated enemy before the world and to impede the development of the German people for all time."

So Ludendorff turned his attention to the next German offensive of 1918, that of July. He complained that there was a great leakage of important military information and that deserters had become a problem. The drive started on the 15th, but after initial successes all sorts of difficulties arose. Certain divisions did badly indeed and for the first time Ludendorff began to talk of the sharp attacks by Marshal Foch. Influenza added to the difficulties of the German High Command. Then came the story of the German withdrawal front the Marne. Ludendorff wrote:

The attempt to make the nations of the Entente inclined to peace before the arrival of the American reinforcements by means of German victories had failed. The energy of the army had not sufficed to deal the enemy a decisive blow before the Americans were on the spot in considerable force. It was quite clear to me that our general situation had thus become very serious.

Then came Aug. 8, which Ludendorff said "was the black day of the German Army in the history of this war." With the Germans planning a withdrawal, the British and French attacked in the region of Albert and succeeded in making a deep break through the German lines. This forced a general German withdrawal in the whole district.

Ludendorff wrote: "Aug. 8 put the decline of that fighting power beyond all doubt…. The war must be ended."

On the next page, he recorded the following: "The Emperor told me later that after the failure of the July offensive and after Aug. 8, he knew that the war could no longer be won."

Ludendorff's book then mixes the story of the Allied drive against the German front in the latter part of August and in September with the story of efforts of the Germans to stage gracefully the defeat which he foresaw. There were talks of appealing to the Vatican, to the Queen of Holland and to Wilson. Things did not move swiftly enough to suit Ludendorff, who feared that Austria-Hungary would negotiate a separate peace and thus leave Germany in a worse position.

After reviewing a series of German reverses, Ludendorff recorded this impression as of Sept. 9: "In these circumstances I felt compelled to undertake the responsible task of hastening the end of the war."

There ensued much discussion in Berlin with which Ludendorff found great fault on the ground that there was a lack of unity and "treason" in the air. So much so, that he recorded: "At 6 o'clock on the evening of Sept. 28 I went down to the Field Marshal's room, which was one floor below mine. I explained to him my views as to a peace offer and a request for an armistice…. The Field Marshal listened to me with emotion. He answered that he had intended to say the same thing to me in the evening, that he had considered the situation carefully and thought the step necessary."

On Sept. 29 it was decided to ask President Wilson to arrange an armistice and peace. On Oct. 2. Major Baron von dem Busch, representing the German General Staff, addressed the leaders of the Reichstag and in his speech said:

"We can carry on the war for a substantial further period, we can cause the enemy further heavy losses, we can lay waste his country as we retire, but we can-not win." Then the major relayed the demand of the General Staff that the war be ended.

The speech caused consternation in Berlin. A government crisis ensued and with it delay which worried Ludendorff not a little. When the new government was formed on Oct. 3, it had placed before it at once a letter from Von Hindenburg which read:

General Headquarters holds to the demand made by it on Monday, Sept. 29, of this year, for an immediate offer of peace to the enemy. ...

In these circumstances the only right course is to give up the fight, in order to spare useless sacrifices of the German people and their Allies. Every day wasted costs the lives of thousands of brave German soldiers.

Interestingly enough, in all the pages telling of the German effort to stage a peace, Ludendorff had made no mention of Wilson's Fourteen Points except the following:

In a telegram on Oct. 2, I emphasized that the Fourteen Points of the Wilson note were to serve as the basis for the discussion of peace terms but were not to be regarded as conditions imposed on us by the enemy.

And Wilson's Fourteen Points had been published eight months before!

The first note went to Wilson and his reply was received on Oct. 9. It called for the evacuation of France, to which there was no great objection in Germany. But other conditions caused much discussion in which Ludendorff found heaped upon him much blame for the débâcle of the German war machine.

In the meanwhile Allied victories on the front made the German situation worse. Ludendorff told of starting the construction of defense lines along the German frontier.

Then came Wilson's second note, which dismayed the Germans. They contended that in the accusations made by Wilson there was the hand of Clemenceau and Lloyd George. Ludendorff wrote that it seemed to be a case of having to decide whether to surrender unconditionally to the Allies or to continue to fight under most unfavorable conditions, especially in view of the bad political conditions within Germany.

Ludendorff then became deeply involved in the debates. He found Wilson's terms too harsh and began to talk of continuing the fight for honor's sake. This brought the charge from some Reichstag quarters that he had changed his mind. It was plain that what irked Ludendorff was Wilson's insistence that the armistice should be so arranged that there would be no possibility of Germany's resuming hostilities.

When Wilson's next note arrived, on Oct. 24, leaving it plain that a surrender was demanded, Ludendorff went so far to write: "In my mind there could no longer be doubt in any mind that we must continue to fight."

On Oct. 25, von Hindenburg and Ludendorff saw the Kaiser at Berlin and advised him to go on fighting, rather than accept Wilson's terms. The Kaiser was non-committal, but Ludendorff recorded that the Cabinet seemed hostile to him and von Hindenburg.

Then Ludendorff put it this way: "In the German note of Oct. 27, we capitulated." Two days later he resigned.

The world knows the story of the fortnight of negotiations which followed, ending in the signing of the Armistice on Nov. 11.

So we have Ludendorff's story of how the war ended. Through 300 pages of his second volume he reviews the weakening of the German Army, the growth of disaffection at home and repeats over and over how he and von Hindenburg advised that Germany could not win. True enough, he weakened at the last moment in the face of his responsibilities, but that does not affect the story he told of Germany's military defeat. He had made the record and the record showed that the Kaiser's armies were beaten.

What is more: The record as made by Ludendorff shows that Wilson's Fourteen Points were not "seized upon" by the German people in the hope of a peace of compromise. The Kaiser, von Hindenburg and Ludendorff all bore testimony to the fact that Germany knew she was surrendering. She was surrendering because she was beaten and all the talk of violation of the promises Wilson made her is mere special pleading.

Hitler says Germany was not beaten in 1918. Who should know — the Quartermaster General or the blinded infantry corporal?

The Fuehrer's commander and his own associate in later days had made him out the liar that he is.

Hitler Vows a Finish Fight, Warns Dissidents of Death

BY THE NEW YORK TIMES | NOV. 9, 1943

BERNE, SWITZERLAND, NOV. 8 — On the twentieth anniversary of the National Socialist revolution — and on the eve of the twenty-fifth anniversary of the German armistice parleys in World War I — Adolf Hitler once again foregathered with the faithful in the Loewenbrau beer cellar in Munich, tonight.

In a 45-minute speech, he declared that Germany would fight on determinedly — come what may. His own nerves, he averred, were strong and steady and his confidence in the German masses was unshaken. He was certain, he said, that every man and woman in Germany would answer the call to arms if war threatened the German frontier.

Hitler and associates celebrate the twentieth anniversary of the 1923 Beer Hall Putsch in the Löwenbräukeller beer hall in Munich, Germany on Nov. 9, 1943.

No quarter, therefore, would be conceded to defeatists at home, he warned, and that those who speculated on an Allied victory for reasons of personal gain would be summarily destroyed.

At a time when tens of thousands of German soldiers were risking their lives on the fighting fronts — this admission of risk was a new departure for Hitler — the Reich would not boggle over the elimination of internal criminals, he warned.

In promising vengeance for the Allied bombing of the Reich cities Hitler said:

> Thank God that although we cannot reach America today I have one opponent within reach [meaning Britain] and will exact retribution from him.

His speech was a summons for concentration on the home front of faith in ultimate victory and an exhortation to give the fighting troops the moral backing that is their due.

"If the German people despair," he said at another point, "they will deserve no better than they get. If they despair I will not be sorry for them if God lets them down."

He made no apologies for the familiar encomiums that marked his previous references to the Russian campaign.

His complete omission of all explanation for the German breakdown in the east was conspicuous. The summary manner in which he generalized in his references to future military operations was also noticeable.

The Wehrmacht, he warned, was prepared to meet an enemy landing wherever it might be attempted.

A brief but sympathetic reference to the victims of enemy air raids was supplemented by the warning that retaliation would follow.

He had promised President Roosevelt, he added with a note of disillusionment, that Germany would not employ bombers or heavy fighters, but he had since discovered, he said, that the promise had only been exacted to give Germany's enemies time to perfect their own aerial armament.

Familiar retrospective references to 1918 were not lacking entirely from the speech, however. The Weimar Republic, he said, was systematically tortured to death after President Woodrow Wilson's 14-point peace program. Financial and economic exploitation by the "benevolent democracies" administered its coup de grâce.

Post-war reconstruction programs were presently being bandied about, he said, and he suggested that their protagonists would do well to begin their social reforms at home. National Socialism, he said, would take care of the rebuilding of Germany.

The speech contained no reference to outlook for peace or predictions as to possible duration of the war. The "Bolshevist Colossus," he said, would not rest until it had dominated Europe. For the present, he went on, Germany alone was warding it off with the might of her arms.

A brief reference to the "treachery" of the King of Italy constituted practically his only mention of the Italian collapse. Another was: "the collapse of Italy won't fail to influence the further course of events … but enemy expectations have not been realized." His boasted "storming" of the Brenner has now resolved itself into an offensive south of Rome which is presently proceeding at a snail's pace.

Concluding, he thundered:

Germany won't lapse into the errors of 1918 by capitulating and any enemy speculation to that effect will be disproved.

Among prominent party members attending tonight's festivities, such as they were, were Reich Marshal Hermann Goering, Dr. Joseph Goebbels, Propaganda Minister; Heinrich Himmler, Gestapo Chief and Minister of Interior; and Dr. Robert Ley, head of the German Labor Front.

Hitler's Last Arguments

BY THE NEW YORK TIMES | JAN. 31, 1944

INTRODUCED by an hour's overture of Wagnerian music as his only iden-
tification, Adolf Hitler has delivered another speech. The occasion was
the eleventh anniversary of that day of infamy on which treachery to
all that was best in Germany and in our civilization brought Hitler
and his foul gang to power. And the place from which this customary
anniversary speech was broadcast was not the ruined German capital, where he and his cohorts used to strut, but Hitler's hidden headquarters, where he presumably felt himself safe from Allied bombs.
The musical selections have not been announced, but they fell short
of historic fitness if they failed to include the swan song in which the
Wagnerian knight whom Hitler fancied himself to be bids farewell to
the world of men and women. For if the confident predictions of General Eisenhower and other authoritative spokesmen are realized, this
was Hitler's last anniversary speech, and the much-enduring world
will not have to concern itself with another.

In point of fact, that was also the leitmotif which Hitler struck. There
was no longer any confident prediction of victory. "Victory," said Hitler,
"is not an article of faith, but an innermost certainty." In other words,
one more of those Hitlerian intuitions that are now at a great discount.
And what could this man tell his disillusioned people? They see their
ruined cities; they feel the moral and physical exhaustion of the war;
they know that defeat is staring them in the face; and they dread the
vengeance of an outraged world. National Socialism, says Hitler in his
defense, has solved all social and economic problems and established
equality of opportunity. To the war-weary Germans that must sound
like supreme mockery. For Hitler solved the social problems by ruthless murder and regimentation. He solved the economic problems by
a reckless plunge into war preparations. And the only opportunity and
equality he established is the opportunity of loot for the leaders and the

equality of death for the masses. The only promise he can make them now is further "pain and suffering." The only appeal he has left is to warn them of the coming punishment in case of defeat.

There is no denying, however, that for a man in his desperate position Hitler made the most of arguments which might still appeal to some Germans and some Europeans. "In this struggle," he said, "there can be only one victor, and that will be either Germany or Soviet Russia." And he proceeds to warn all and sundry of the terrible consequences of a Russian victory, and what it would mean to the European states which he crushed under his heel and to European civilization, which he has befouled. He tells Great Britain and the United States that the Bolsheviks will get them, while at the same time suggesting to Russia that Britain will lead the fight against Russia after this war. He mocks the conquered nations that Britain's promised aid was ineffective, and he taunts the British Dominion soldiers that they are fighting England's battles. Finally he does his best to hurl renewed anti-Semitic propaganda in the midst of all of them.

This is, of course, his old method of divide and rule. It helped him to conquer Germany before the war and to conquer Europe in the war. Most of these arguments will only raise derisive laughter among those to whom they are addressed. As for his principal argument, the role which Russia will play after victory, it should be obvious even to him that after the conferences of Moscow and Teheran the remaining differences between Russia and the Western allies can no longer affect the conduct or the outcome of the war.

But a drowning man grabs at straws, and his argument will be echoed by other drowning men among his satellites. The one conclusive answer to it is, of course, the demonstration that there is an alternative to Hitler's policy of rule or ruin — namely, cooperation. A firm basis for such cooperation between Russia, Great Britain, China and the United States has already been painstakingly laid, and they are pledged to continue it in war and peace. But the way to begin cooperation is to cooperate, and on the manner in which that cooperation develops will depend the effectiveness of Hitler's argument in the future.

Hitler's Last Victories

BY THE NEW YORK TIMES | MARCH 23, 1944

ADOLF HITLER is celebrating his last victories these days. Unable to conquer his foes, he is conquering his allies. This is being done with the same treachery and ruthlessness, but also with the same decisive speed and display of power, that overwhelmed many European nations in the past. His conquest of Hungary appears to be complete, and now his troops are reported to be marching on to establish an equally complete occupation of Slovakia, Rumania and Bulgaria.

Nor is there much to stop them. Like Mussolini's Italy and Horthy's Hungary, these countries have dispersed their own troops to fight Germany's battles and have lost much not only in manpower but especially in matériel, for which they are completely dependent on Germany. The German fifth column and native Nazis are crushing potential opposition even before the German troops spread out. This is indicated again by broadcast orders to all Germans in Rumania to put themselves at the disposal of the German army, which is already solidly entrenched in the country, Slovakia is too small to be a military factor. And though Bulgaria, which has followed a more independent policy and in particular refused to join in the war against Russia, might prove a harder nut to crack, its home forces are scarcely in a position to offer much resistance.

The Germans explain that they are taking measures to establish "equality of sacrifice" and to "intensify the military and political collaboration between Germany and her allies." That is a propagandistic euphemism designed to cover up the fact that German militarism is crushing the last vestiges of independence within its sphere of operations and that the small nations which elected to go with Germany either because of greed or because of a mistaken choice of the lesser evil are now paying for it with their existence. It is a warning which Finland, for one, should heed while it still has a chance to do so. For "intensified collaboration" is merely an ominous paraphrase of Goebbels' previous declaration that nobody will be permitted to escape; and "equality of sacrifice" can only mean that all the nations within the German orbit will now be called upon to sacrifice all their manhood and all their substance in a final mad dance of death around the Wagnerian funeral pyre.

For easy as Hitler's last victories may turn out to be, they are also his last desperate measures to stave off the doom that is closing in on him. With half his army and most of his air force either engaged or immobilized in the west and a great force retreating under pressure of the Russian armies, he is compelled to spread his remaining forces even more thinly than before and risk turning former friends into new enemies. The collapse of the Balkans was the signal of the approaching German collapse in the last war. Hitler, confronted with the unmistakable war weariness and peace efforts of all his satellites, is determined to prevent such a collapse in 1944.

At the same time, it would be folly to ignore that in the long diplomatic battle for the Balkans Hitler has; for the moment at least, obtained a draw, if he loses the active support of the

Balkan states he is also keeping them from going over to the Allied camp. A divided and irresolute Allied diplomacy has been matched by Hitler's armed force. The result is the tramp of the German army in the Balkans.

Hitler's Fifty-Five Years

BY THE NEW YORK TIMES | APRIL 20, 1944

ADOLF HITLER was born 55 years ago today in the town of Braunau on the Inn, near the German border of Austria. We cannot positively say that everything would be well in the world if he had not been born, but we can be fairly sure that things would not be worse than they are. We do not have to go outside the pages of "Mein Kampf" to understand why he became what he did. His father was a peasant boy who by terrific exertions had worked up in middle life to the position of a small civil servant. The father died when Adolf was 13. Five years later Adolf's mother died, leaving no property, and at 18 the boy, as he later said, "was faced with the problem of earning his daily bread." It appears that he had done nothing to earn any bread as long as the family funds held out.

He went to Vienna to make his fortune, first working as a laborer in the building trades, then making and selling what he called "aquarelles." He was thoroughly miserable. "Vienna, the city that to so many represents the idea of harmless gaiety, the festive place for merry-making," he later wrote, "is to me only the living memory of the most miserable time of my life." He also wrote, not specifically of himself, but the words do apply: "He loiters about hungrily, he pawns or sells the last of his belongings, his clothes get shabbier day by day, and he sinks into surroundings which, apart from the material misery he experiences, also poison his spirit." He was a wretched, disappointed young man, and but of the wretchedness came his lifelong hates — of successful people, of independent labor unions, of liberalism, of Jews.

His happier days began when, as he relates, he went to Munich in 1912: two years of relative well-being, four years in a Bavarian regiment in which his official record was good if not brilliant, the beginnings of the Nazi party. But the gnawing sense of failure bred in the

Vienna days never left him. It twisted his life. Because Hitler — and, of course, a great many other misfits — had this sense of failure, Germany had to be barbarized and the world plunged into the most dreadful of wars. Four years ago Hitler and his friends didn't look or feel like failures. Maybe they didn't two years ago. Now the old feeling must be coming back. The spirit that was poisoned in Vienna between 1908 and 1912 is being poisoned again — this time by an advancing Russian army, by thousands of Allied planes and by the prospect of invasion and disaster. It can't be much of a birthday for that distorted little soul.

Hitler's Last Weapon

BY THE NEW YORK TIMES | JULY 3, 1944

AFTER A LONG SILENCE during which Germany's impending catastrophe has been made evident to all, including the Germans themselves, Adolf Hitler has again found the courage to raise his voice in a speech. It was only fitting that this first speech after the Allied invasion of France, the fall of Rome end the new German disaster in Russia which initiate the final Allied offensive against Berlin, should have been a funeral oration. Its somber mood helped him to cover up the significance of his enforced admission that after nearly five years of wanton war Germany finds herself confronted with a "difficult situation" and a "time of crisis" which other German propagandists have already characterized as the approach of Germany's "last hour or her last chance." But there is even more significance in two other points he made in his speech. The first is that after the failure of all his other weapons, Hitler is falling back on the one weapon which he has always considered as being uniquely his own — namely, fanaticism. The second is that he should have extolled the object of his funeral oration, Gen. Eduard Dietl, the Nazi commander in Finland, as a special prop of his own position, "a prop above all in the German officer corps," adding to this an exhortation to other German officers to follow the dead general's example.

It is strange that in this age of reason, so often accused of lack of faith, political fanaticism should have become rampant throughout large parts of the world, giving this war a particularly savage character. And it is especially strange that a howling political dervish like Hitler should have been able to implant in a large section of the German people the same kind of fanaticism which is natural and comprehensible in Japan, whose political, social and religious roots still stick in darkest savagery, but which seems wholly out of place in Europe. Yet there is no denying Hitler's success, and to this fanaticism Hitler now makes his last appeal. "How," he exclaims, "could a struggle which has behind it all the fanaticism of a nation end otherwise than in victory!" But it is this fanaticism which, in the last analysis, led both Germany and Japan on the road to disaster and insures their doom.

For this fanaticism made these nations blind, and their blindness could only lead to the abyss. Deliberately cultivated fanaticism enabled their leaders to train their youth to blind obedience and suicidal death; but however effective it proved in the beginning, it is now proving a serious handicap which only lifts their total battle losses. What is more important, it made them blind to the real nature of the world about them and to the moral forces which their fanaticism was bound to raise against them. It made them blind to the grim courage of the British, and to the heroism of the Russian people in defense of their own soil. It made them blind to the faith and determination of America that merely awaited the full realization of the challenge to go into action. It made them blind to the endurance of the Chinese. And it made them blind to the counterfanaticism which their own fanaticism was bound to arouse in those they hoped to crush — in the Poles, and the French, and the Yugoslavs, and the Greeks, and the Norwegians, and the Dutch, and the Belgians, and now, finally, even in the supposedly quiescent Danes, who are the first nation to rise up against Hitler in their whole mass and defy the conqueror right in their own capital.

Whether free or still under the Nazi heel, the angered forces of humanity are on the march, and before their anger Nazi fanaticism is already beginning to wilt. And that explains Hitler's appeal to the German officers. For while these officers are willing enough to let the Nazi fanatics fight to the death, they are no longer willing to die for Hitler themselves, as shown by the German commander of Cherbourg. And their growing lack of confidence is obviously beginning to affect the German troops, who, awakening from their trance, are beginning to surrender in droves. But the growing conviction, of the German generals that the war is lost is the most direct threat to Hitler himself. It begins to shatter the most important prop that keeps him in power — a prop which even the Gestapo cannot replace.

Hitler's Last Kampf

BY THE NEW YORK TIMES | SEPT. 22, 1944

SURROUNDED ON ALL SIDES by victorious armies and vengeful populations, forsaken by virtually all his allies and satellites, Adolf Hitler, the man who set out to conquer the world, is fighting his last battle. Into it he is pouring the life-blood and the last physical and moral resources of the German people, emulating in a different sense the maxim of another absolute ruler, "After us the deluge." With the flower of German manhood buried in distant graves or herded into Allied prison camps, old men and boys are now filling up the depleted army ranks, interspersed with fanatical Nazis to keep them in line. Women and slave laborers work his war factories under the supervision of the Gestapo. The whole nation has been stripped bare of all materials capable of bolstering up the war machine. Finally, the last moral forces around which the German people might rally after Hitler are systematically being destroyed at home, and their last moral claims to the consideration of the victors are being dissipated by continued atrocities.

The reports from the various fronts are proof, that this fight is a grim and bitter business. The Allies still need all the strength they can bring to bear on every battlefield to win it. But Hitler's eastern lines are breaking before the Russian onslaughts at Tallinn, Riga, Warsaw, and points south. His Balkan armies are in peril of being trapped. His Gothic Line in Italy has been pierced and is in danger of collapse. His vaunted Westwall is still a major obstacle to Allied progress, and fierce battles are being fought in front of it and within its fortress zones. But this obstacle too is being circumvented by the Allied flanking movement through the Netherlands, where in epic and desperate battles encircled airborne troops secured the bridges of the lower Rhine and, vaulting across supposedly impregnable water barriers, opened up a new invasion path into the heart of Germany.

The German armies at the fronts now represent the last hard shell of the Third Reich. Beyond that shell there is nothing that could successfully resist an Allied march to Berlin.

Hitler's Home Guard

BY THE NEW YORK TIMES | OCT. 19, 1944

IN A PROCLAMATION which confesses his military and political bankruptcy, Adolf Hitler, self-styled Fuehrer of all Germans, who set out to conquer the world for the German "master race," has now appealed to the German people to rise in one last mobilization of young and old to defend the borders of their own land.

With his Reich besieged on all sides and invaded from two, "the greatest war lord of all times," who once boasted of the mightiest armies in the world and sent them marching from the Arctic to Africa, and from the Caucasus to the Atlantic, has now been forced to order the formation of a Home Guard of boys and old men who are expected to halt the forces of avenging justice which his armies are unable to stop. The Messiah of a New Order and a "Germanic era" has at last been forced to confess that after five years of war, Germany stands "alone" against a solid bloc of enemies. And it is characteristic of the Nazi mentality that the men who shot guerrilla fighters on sight throughout Europe as "franctireurs" and beyond even military law, should now claim the rights of warfare for their own Home Guard.

It is an interesting commentary that Hitler should have chosen the anniversary of the Battle of Nations at Leipzig in 1813 to announce his last defense program. For in that battle another war lord, Napoleon, who also sought to conquer the world, was defeated by the combined forces of many nations fighting for freedom from his domination. The comparison between Napoleon and Hitler has been made so often that all Germans must recognize the parallel between the Battle of Leipzig and the present battle of Germany. But even that parallel is no longer exact. At Leipzig Napoleon still fought for victory. Hitler, by his own proclamation, no longer dares even to mention victory, much less world conquest. He merely calls for a desperate defense until "a peace is guaranteed which safeguards the future of Germany." What he means is a peace which safeguards the future of himself and the Nazi regime. Hitler, the ex-Austrian lance corporal, is willing to defend his life to the last German.

What results can be expected from this last desperate measure? There is little doubt that the control of the Nazis is still strong enough to organize the Home Guard as planned. But in a comparison with the German army forces already beaten in the field, the military value of such an organization cannot be great. Neither the German character nor the German landscape is adapted to guerrilla warfare. That the Nazi fanatics will want to continue fighting is certain, but the Germans fight well only in formation under strictly "legal" command, and even Nazi fanaticism has been known to ebb under the impact of defeat. As for the large majority of the German people, it seems doubtful whether they have either the moral stamina or the traditions of liberty that inspired the British Home Guard and the guerrilla fighters of oppressed Europe. They know that Hitler's last call to arms can no longer avert defeat. It can only devastate the country further and take another heavy toll of German lives.

Hitler Mystery Adds
to Uneasy Reich's Woes

BY GEORGE AXELSSON | NOV. 19, 1944

STOCKHOLM, SWEDEN, NOV. 18 — Adolf Hitler's silence on the Nov. 9 anniversary of the Munich beer-hall putsch opened wide the sluice gates of speculation as to what might lie behind this sudden and dramatic departure from a 21-year-old Nazi tradition.

Is Hitler sick, shelved, on his way to Japan in a submarine or even dead, are some of the questions being asked in the Reich as well as in the rest of the world because of his failure to speak to his people on Nov. 9. The substitution of the traditional Munich speech by a proclamation allegedly written by Hitler and read by Gestapo Chief Heinrich Himmler in an apparently makeshift ceremony on Nov. 12, meant to reassure the German people, only added to the feeling of uneasiness in the country and provided a fresh impulse for guessers.

In Stockholm we have been overrun by rumor merchants, each claiming to have the inside story. It has been pretty much like buying a racetrack tip and no more reliable. It is interesting that no two of the stories put out here by persons pretending to know the truth are identical.

DENOUEMENT LIKELY SOON

One thing can be deduced from what has happened, or rather from what did not happen: Either it was politically inconvenient that Hitler speak on the beer-hall putsch day or he was physically unable to do so. Whether one or the other is the correct explanation, it is a grave development for Nazi Germany, the repercussions of which should not be long in becoming known to the outside world.

Nothing that has come out of Berlin recently furnishes an answer to the many questions forcing themselves upon observers because of the canceled Munich speech and the Hitler-signed and Himmler-read proclamation. A situation evidently has arisen in which it has been judged best to dispense with Hitler speeches, not to mention personal appearances, but the whys and wherefores of this new situation remain a mystery.

It is true Goebbels has said Hitler was too busy with military affairs to bother with making speeches, but he has not explained why Hitler could not spare 20 minutes for a recorded speech in lieu of that proclamation.

The Gestapo chief has always been known as 100 percent loyal to Hitler, who he believes is needed for the political stability of the Nazi regime. But if a situation comes up to make Himmler doubt the usefulness of continued loyalty the Gestapo chief is not above repudiating his nominal master.

HIMMLER AS MASTER

That may be what is taking place today. Rather than sell out to a new master it is quite conceivable that Himmler has decided to become his own master, as in practice he already is. To himself he can justify treason by the fact that he is the representative of the most fanatical elements in the Elite Guard and Gestapo — desperadoes who like himself have no choice and are determined to sell their lives as dearly as possible, regardless of the cost to the German nation.

If there be any reason other than ill health making Hitler's removal from the Nazi stage an urgent necessity in Himmler's view, it is the military and political setbacks of the last two years. These reverses have already imposed many restrictions on Hitler's authority and a gradual transfer of his powers to Himmler,

The desire to isolate Hitler may in fact have originated in these circles eager to insure a succession for a ruthless Nazi like Himmler and to remove "softer" leaders like Goering, who officially serves as Hitler's successor. Himmler needs the support and advice of these higher-up Nazis, and it is not unlikely that he has been forced by them to drop Hitler.

"STRENGTH THROUGH FEAR"

At one time Reinhard Heydrich was Himmler's chief adviser. Now it is Gen. Ernst Kaltenbrunner and an SS [Elite Guard] leader calling himself Wulff, which may or may not be an assumed name. Many top Gestapo men work under pseudonyms. This pair and all like them in the Reich constitute a group whose slogan today is "Strength Through Fear." Without them Himmler cannot rule, so it would not be surprising if he has forsworn his allegiance to Hitler in their favor.

The stage appears all set for Hitler's exit, but Himmler and his fellow top Nazis are determined that the departure shall not make any difference in the conduct of the war nor in Germany's internal affairs other than in the direction of a further increased effort to mobilize even more completely their resources, if at all possible.

How the German people will react to Hitler's removal is, of course, a factor that needs to be reckoned with, but they were told in Sunday's proclamation not only that objectors would be pitilessly exterminated but also, through measures stretched over a long period, that Himmler has gradually placed the people in a position where they must like it or swing for it.

FIRMER STAND SOUGHT

As for the army, survivors of the July purge probably can be depended on to continue the fight, no matter what happens to Hitler. Judging by the workmanlike way in which the retreat has been operated, both in the east and in the west, Hitler has not had anything to do with the Wehrmacht for a long time and would not be missed too much there. Neither the Wehrmacht nor the party would find it difficult to transfer allegiance to Himmler, especially since they know the penalty that the Gestapo would mete out for protests.

The sum total of those observations therefore is that the shelving of Hitler offers no prospect of precipitating a German collapse, nor does it hold out any hope to the Germans of an imminent cave-in of nazism.

On the contrary, it may prove true what Goebbels had occasion to say recently only in other words, that only from now on will the people of Germany get a taste of what real nazism is like.

Hitler Bids Reich Die for Nazi Tenets

BY THE NEW YORK TIMES | JAN. 31, 1945

LONDON, JAN. 30 — Adolf Hitler, broadcasting from his headquarters on the twelfth anniversary of his accession to power, told the German people tonight that he expected them to die in their tracks working or fighting for the preservation of National Socialism.

Although earlier the microphone had been at the disposal of dispensers of gloom who told their listeners that Stettin, Frankfort on the Oder and even Berlin were threatened with becoming front-line cities, Hitler sought to convince the Germans that by maintaining unity they still had a chance for "final victory" and that in continuing their resistance they were fulfilling their moral destiny of preserving Europe from domination by what he termed the Asiatic-Bolshevist tide.

Ranging from Versailles through the period between the Nazis' rise to power and the outbreak of the war, Hitler's speech followed the familiar pattern of self-justification, threats and promises. Unlike his earlier orations, it lasted barely 20 minutes, and while it was unquestionably he who spoke, it fell short of his earlier efforts at abuse of the Allies' leaders and, except in parts, it was a poor shadow of the frenzy he used to muster for his perorations.

Sometimes his words were hard to distinguish. This was not due entirely to his bad [Austrian] German but to the faintness of reception, indicating that the broadcast came over long land wires, necessitating "boosting" at several points.

Hitler spent a good deal of effort apparently trying to convince the Germans that the perils they faced by continuing the war were less than those they would face if they met the Allies' demand for unconditional surrender.

This has been the line laid down by Propaganda Minister Joseph Goebbels for some time, Prime Minister Churchill tried to undermine it as far as he was able to do in his last speech when he said that the

Allies' treatment of a conquered Germany would be governed by the rules of civilized behavior followed in Allied countries.

There were passages in Hitler's speech that rather suggested fear that this Churchillian pronouncement might be followed by some definite announcement after the meeting of Mr. Churchill, Premier Stalin and President Roosevelt.

He said that in the democracies "political activities and lies are inextricably linked" and declared that promises of the Western democracies were without value because they were powerless to enforce them against the wishes of Moscow.

All the small European countries that left Germany's side trusting in the Allies' promises, he said, were doomed to "complete annihilation," whether it came now or later. He said Germany would never suffer that fate because of the unity he gave to the Reich when he took over control 12 years ago in an era of unemployment, economic discrimination, financial distress and what he termed a Bolshevist menace that he pictured as hardly less terrifying than that of today.

CHAPTER 6

The Fuehrer's Death and Legacy

On April 30, 1945, Adolf Hitler committed suicide by gunshot in his war bunker in Berlin. Incredulity and intrigue were common responses to the news of the death of one of the era's greatest villains. Following his death and interviews with his closest confidantes after the war, reports detailed the curiosities of Hitler's mind and habits. To this day, few fail to be fascinated by the psychology of Hitler. His life is a cautionary tale of the destruction a politician can cause when economic concerns and xenophobia stoke fear in the hearts of the people, and few stand to resist him.

City Takes Report of Death in Stride

BY MEYER BERGER | MAY 2, 1945

REPORTS OF Adolf Hitler's death, like the weather yesterday, left New Yorkers cold. They stopped only briefly in the chill rain of the evening rush hour to glance at headlines, to shrug in disbelief, before they dived like moles into the subway.

Skepticism was by far the dominant reaction. There was no cheering, only subdued gloating. The comparative few who discussed the reports aloud seemed to find profane speech most fitting. Eight of ten persons took the attitude: "It's another Nazi fake," or, "They're trying to palm off a Hitler double."

Though the reports broke here a little before 5 P. M., they filtered as slowly as winter molasses through rain-swept Times Square. A police sergeant from Traffic J moved from Forty-second Street to the Times Tower's bulletin board at Forty-third Street to verify oral rumor.

Beaded rain dripped from his cap as he stared at the poster: "Hitler Is Dead." He shook off the rain. He said: "So the bum's dead, eh?" and, as if answering his own question, he said dully: "What difference does it make now?"

FRENCH SAILORS BITTER

Two French sailors read the sign. One turned to sodden civilians grouped near him. He said: "It is the end of the pig. He will roast in hell." The civilians looked bewildered. They remained silent.

A bobby-socks blonde turned to a friend and repeated the legend on the bulletin board. Her friend tugged at her sleeve to hurry her on. She said: "Too bad he's dead. He should have been tortured."

A tall Italian told them: "Do not believe what it says. Believe it when you see a picture of Hitler as you saw Mussolini's picture yesterday." The girls moved off without reply.

Skepticism took some amusing turns. A sharp-featured woman told a friend sharing her umbrella: "Don't believe what bulletins tell you. This morning the bulletin said: 'light showers today.' "

The appearance of newspaper extras started a sudden flurry. Hoarse cries of "Hitler dies — get that uxtray!" brought surging groups to newsstands and the hucksters' cries added to the traffic din, but only for a while. Within an hour, extras found few buyers.

Leo Kaplan of 32-15 Forty-first Street, Astoria, Queens, a soldier hit by machine-gun bullets in the Philippines, hobbled across the Square through the downpour. He stopped to say: "If it's true, it's the greatest thing I ever heard."

A mounted policeman, huddled glumly under his rubber cape, waited until the soldier was beyond earshot. He said: "It would have been good news 20 years ago. Late now." He stared gloomily eastward down Forty-second Street.

The East Side gave no more outward evidence of gloating or belief in the report than did Yorkville, traditional German quarter. The same was general true in all the city's Jewish districts.

Service men were outspoken. Lieut. Arthur McIntyre of Kansas City, Mo., an air corps man, said in Times Square when he saw the bulletin: "Good riddance." Sgt. John Eliopoulos of Haverhill, Mass., an Army engineer, remarked bitterly in Pennsylvania Station: "We'd like to spit on his grave, the ———." He spoke for a group of five.

Joe Ente, who owns a monument yard at 89 Ludlow Street, discussed the report in terms of his trade. He said: "His headstone should be a skunk. But he shouldn't be buried. He will contaminate the good earth."

CHINATOWN SKEPTICAL

Chinatown took the news gravely, but skeptically, like the rest of the city. Shavey Lee, its mayor, said fervently: "Here's hoping we can sing the death of Hirohito."

Commuters bound home through the murky twilight read the scant details of Hitler's reported end and stared moodily but silently at drear landscape. Out in the Brownsville district of Brooklyn, Joe Sisselman, who works in Hoffman's Cafeteria at Saratoga and Pitkin Avenues, looked up from a mound of dishes when he heard the report. "Maybe," he said, "it will save the lives of some of our American kids. For me it comes late."

His son, Leonard Sisselman, was reported dead in Germany 10 days ago. He had been with the Ninetieth Division of the Third Army.

Rabbi Henry A. Schorr of 1100 Grand Concourse, the Bronx, said: "He leaves behind him a ruined and agonized world, the monument to his madness. God save humanity from the seeds of his tyranny and terror."

Mayor La Guardia was returning from Brooklyn where he had helped to open a city health center, when he was informed of Hitler's reported death. "That's the best news I've heard," he shouted into the two-way police radio in his car. "Look for anything to happen now."

Broken Promises Fill Hitler Record

BY THE NEW YORK TIMES | MAY 2, 1945

HITLER'S RECORD of broken promises stands out as one of the conspicuous features of his career.

When he first came into power the question of most immediate concern to Europe was that of the Saar Basin, the part of Germany held by France and administered by the League of Nations in accordance with the Versailles Treaty for 15 years. After that period the people of the Saar were to vote on whether they desired to return to Germany, become part of France or remain under the League.

Speaking in the Reichstag on Jan. 30, 1934, on the Saar issue, which was becoming acute because of the approaching plebiscite, Hitler said:

> After the solution of this question, the German Government is willing and determined to accept in its innermost soul, as well as external formulation, the Pact of Locarno.

MARCH INTO RHINELAND

On March 1, 1935, after the plebiscite, in which Germany received more than 90 percent of the votes, sovereignty over the region was returned to Germany. One year later German troops marched into the Rhineland zone created by the Treaty of Versailles and guaranteed against remilitarization by the Locarno pact entered into voluntarily by Germany in 1925.

To reassure Europe as to his purpose in marching into the Rhineland, Hitler declared:

> I have removed the question of the everlasting European revision of frontiers from the atmosphere of public discussion in Germany.

He gave this assurance in a speech in the Reichstag: "After three years I believe I can today regard the struggle for German equality as over. We have no territorial demands to make in Europe."

Speaking again in the Reichstag, this time on the Austrian question, on May 21, 1935, Hitler said:

Germany has neither the wish, nor the intention to mix in internal Austrian affairs or to annex of unite with Austria.

On Jan. 30, 1937, he buttressed this promise by saying:

With this declaration I wish to announce that the era of so-called surprises has been concluded.

Within a little more than a year after these declarations Hitler marched into Austria and incorporated the country in the German Reich.

A week after German troops had driven into Austria Hitler declared:

The eternal dream of the German people has been fulfilled. Germany wants only peace. She does not want to add to the sorrows of other nations.

CONQUEST AFTER CONQUEST

The conquest of Austria was barely two months old when Hitler raised the question of Czechoslovakia by mobilizing and threatening to invade her. On that occasion the Czechs countered with their own mobilization, and Hitler appeared to hold back his blow. But in September, 1938, he raised the question of the annexation of the Sudeten country to Germany, after instigating, as he had in Austria, a state of civil war in that region as an excuse for intervention.

This crisis ended in the Munich pact of Sept. 30, 1938, by which Germany obtained the Sudeten and other German regions of Czechoslovakia.

Referring to a speech made by Hitler in Berlin after he had gone to see him at Berchtesgaden, the visit that led to the Munich pact, Prime

Minister Neville Chamberlain said:

> *He told me privately, and last night he repeated publicly, that after the Sudeten German question is settled, that is the end of Germany's territorial claims in Europe.*

Less than six months after these words were spoken, Hitler marched his troops into Czechoslovakia and reduced the entire country to a German protectorate.

On Jan. 26, 1934, Hitler concluded a 10-year non-aggression treaty with Poland. Under that pact war was absolutely excluded as a means of solving any questions that might arise between the two countries and both nations pledged themselves to maintain the status quo as between the two.

On April 28, 1939, following an address foreshadowing the action, Hitler sent a note to Poland abrogating the treaty and making demands that led on Sept. 1, 1939, to the march of German troops into Poland and the unleashing of the Second World War.

At the time of the abrogation of the treaty with Poland Hitler also informed Great Britain that the naval treaty he had concluded with her on June 13, 1935, limiting the German navy to 35 percent of the British, was null and void. The treaty provided for no such unilateral action. Hitler's sudden invasion of Russia in June, 1941, in violation of his pact with Stalin, was another breach of faith, one that cost him dearly.

Fuehrer Ascetic in Personal Life

BY THE NEW YORK TIMES | MAY 2, 1945

ADOLF HITLER was an ascetic, a celibate and a vegetarian and he neither smoked nor drank. From his early youth he was an eccentric. At the age of 16 he suffered from lung trouble and his passionate ambition to become a great historic figure impelled him to take good care of himself. Careful diet was his deliberately chosen method.

He led a simple life even after he had attained to the dizzy heights of Fuehrer and Chancellor. He had three residences: the official residence in the Chancellor's Palace in Berlin, a modest apartment in Munich and his chalet near Berchtesgaden.

In Berlin he maintained only five servants, carefully chosen from among old party comrades. One of these, Brigadier Schreck, was his chauffeur. The others included his chef, picked for the post because he knew how to cook Hitler's favorite vegetarian dishes and could be relied upon to guard against poisoning; his major-domo and aide-de-camp.

The Fuehrer liked to drive fast in an open automobile and was an aviation enthusiast. When driving he preferred to sit in front with the chauffeur.

HAD A PASSION FOR NEATNESS

His favorite costume consisted of black trousers, khaki coat and neat tie. His only decoration was the Iron Cross he won in the First World War. He disliked jewelry but had a passion for being neat.

Hitler never went shopping and had all the things he wanted to purchase sent to him at the Chancellery.

He suffered from insomnia, and for this reason had no regular hours for going to bed or rising. Luncheon was always promptly at 2 P. M., however. He entertained modestly, the guests usually being party officials and leaders from the provinces. He did not expect his guests to eat his vegetarian food, however, and served their favorite meat and fish dishes. Hitler disliked festive banquets but enjoyed eating out frequently, particularly when in Munich, where he had several haunts. He loved onion soup prepared according to his own recipe.

When in Nuremberg, attending the spectacular Nazi party congresses, he stayed in a modest apartment at the Deutscher Hof, a second-rate hostelry. He shrewdly eschewed personal extravagance as politically unwise.

He was fond of films and liked to give private showings of favorite screen productions before guests at the Chancellery after dinner. He enjoyed looking at newsreels of himself and entertained his guests also with some foreign films. On such occasion he would seat himself on the floor in the dark and appeared to be having a good time.

Although he became the idol of many millions he had no talent for real friendship or intimacy. He had few women friends. His feminine associates, too, were chosen for political purposes. His only passion was politics.

Women of the people did not rally to him until after he had achieved a large degree of prominence. He never became a hero to his valet because he did not have any. Long before housemaids flocked to his support, his feminine supporters were women of the upper class. But he could be very charming to women when he chose and, after achieving power, ever learned the art of kissing their hands in the salon manner. He was not without humor but of a rather heavy sort.

Although he had acquired considerable poise, he was violent in argument.

Hitler made what may be called his social debut in the earlier days of his career in the drawing room of Frau Katherine Hanfstaengl in Munich, but his greatest woman friend was Frau Victoria von Dirksen, widow of a millionaire who built the Berlin subway. She spent a large portion of her husband's fortune in helping to finance Hitler's propaganda. Although in later years she fell out with the party, he continued to regard her as a favorite and for a long time regularly took tea with her at her Berlin home every fortnight.

As a youth Hitler developed a passion for Wagnerian music. In Munich, where he laid the foundations of his movement, he met Frau Winifred Wagner, widow of Siegfried Wagner, the composer's son. Frau Wagner became an enthusiastic Hitlerite and this, together with Hitler's devotion to Wagner, made them fast friends. At one time there were reports that they would marry, but these were denied. Perhaps because of these reports Hitler drew away from her. To Frau Wagner, however, he owed much of his early financial aid. She was not wealthy, but because of her social position she was able to raise considerable sums for the Nazi movement when Hitler most needed money.

Another woman who had his favor was Leni Riefenstahl, a former movie actress, whom he entrusted with the task of editing the propaganda film "The Triumph of Will," the photographing of the 1936 Olympic Games in Berlin and various Nazi meetings and spectacles.

ENGLISH WOMEN HIS FRIENDS

There were also two English women who were his friends, the daughters of Lord Redesdale — the Hon. Diana Freeman-Mitford, a supporter of Sir Oswald Mosley's Blackshirts in England, and the Hon. Unity Freeman-Mitford. The latter was Hitler's favorite and they often lunched together in Munich.

Frau Viorica Ursuleac, a member of the Berlin Opera, also enjoyed Hitler's friendship.

Hitler liked well-dressed women and admired French styles. On one occasion he scotched a movement launched by Frau Joseph Goebbels, wife of the Minister of Propaganda and Enlightenment, for a boycott on French dress models.

Hitler detested evening clothes and wore full dress only on rare visits to the opera.

Though merciless to political opponents, he was kind to animals. A militarist, he was sickened by the sight of blood. A Wagnerian mystic, he loved spectacles of heroics and death. He was simple, Spartan and vain to the point of megalomania. While he took good care of his loyal lieutenants he had no real loyalty to anyone, and in his party he knew how to thwart opposition by setting friends against one another. His enemies he suppressed ruthlessly.

While endowed with vast energy, he was a procrastinator in minor matters and was given to hasty decisions on important things. He talked with great rapidity. An interviewer usually found that it was himself who was being interviewed. While pretending to listen to advice, Hitler always made his own decisions.

He read little, although he possessed a library of 6,000 volumes. His outbursts of furious energy would be preceded by long periods of indolence. When roused to anger, he became dangerous, even for his close associates. He brooked no contradiction. His neurasthenia frequently drove him to tears and hysterics.

Hitler was truly devoted to music not only as an art but as a tonic for his nerves. His favorites were Schubert, Beethoven and Wagner.

One of the many disappointments of his youth was his rejection by the Vienna Academy when he applied for admittance to study art and architecture. He found satisfaction for this rebuff as leader of the Nazi party when he supervised the plans for the Brown House in Munich, party headquarters. He also interfered much in the designing of new museums and Government buildings. To show his appreciation of things beautiful he liked to make gifts of expensively bound books and objects of art.

When the Chancellor's Palace in Berlin was being redecorated for him he superintended the work in several modernistic rooms and paid special attention to the installation of Nordic mythological tapestries depicting Wotan creating the world.

MUNICH HIS FAVORITE CITY

His Munich flat, which he redecorated in 1935 in his favorite baroque blue, white and gold, was in an unfashionable section of the Prinzregentenstrasse. To this flat he would retire when he wanted privacy. Munich was his favorite city, not only because of its architectural beauty but because it was there that his career was launched. The apartment was run by a half-sister, Frau Angela Raubal, who, until her marriage to a Professor Martin Hammitzsch, also supervised Haus Wachenfeld, Hitler's mountain retreat at Berchtesgaden, overlooking a magnificent vista in the Bavarian Alps, at a point from which the Fuehrer could look across into his native Austria.

The Last of Hitler

BY THE NEW YORK TIMES | JUNE 7, 1945

A SMOKE-BLACKENED and charred body found among others in the ruins of the underground fortress beneath the Reich Chancellery in Berlin has been identified with fair certainty by Russian Army physicians as that of Adolf Hitler, who, according to official German accounts, died at 3:30 P. M. May 1, while the Red Army was hammering at the doors of his last hiding place. The Russians have little doubt that they have actually found whatever remains of mankind's greatest enemy, and there can be no real doubt of Hitler's death as such. If final proof were needed, it is supplied by the finding of the bodies of Goebbels and his family near by. Hitler was a fanatic who could hypnotize not only the German masses but himself, and all accounts of the final sessions of the German High Command agree that he had hypnotized himself into making a death stand at Berlin. Goebbels was a cynical careerist who would have gladly fled had he been able to, and if he finally poisoned himself and his family it was only because his master had kept him at his post until it was too late for flight.

The finding of Hitler's body is important because it should put an end to the myths carefully cultivated by some Germans and eagerly snapped up by dime-novel minds abroad that Hitler is still alive and is merely biding his time to reappear and lead the Germans forth to new conquests. Nazism had roots that went far beyond Hitler and dug deep into German history and psychology, but nazism as an organized movement was Hitler's personal creation. Certainly there was nobody else capable of taking his place, as was shown by the complete German collapse immediately after his death. But the myth that he is still alive could well keep the flame of Nazi fanaticism smoldering in some German breasts, to cause future trouble for the Allies.

At the same time, the circumstances of his death and the finding of his body once again emphasize both the ghastly failure and the historic irony of the latest outbreak of the *Furor Teutonicus*. That he should have died, as now appears established, by poison instead of by the sword will undoubtedly be regarded by many Germans as merely a modern improvement on the self-immolation extolled in the legends of primitive Germanic tribes, of which the Japanese hara-kiri is merely an oriental version. But even Germans themselves must be impressed by the sardonic fate which so managed things that the man who tried to conquer the world, who built himself a mighty if hideous chancellery from which to rule the world, should have ended like a rat, in an underground trap, beneath the ruins of his chancellery and amid the wreckage of his capital and his nation, and that all that is left of him is a charred skeleton that cannot even be sufficiently identified for an official death certificate. Thus passes martial glory and ambition as eternal warning to all those who would imitate him.

Hitler Ended Life in Berlin Bunker, British Feel Sure

BY RAYMOND DANIELL | MAY 2, 1945

BERLIN, NOV. 1 — A British major said today that an exhaustive investigation had convinced the British authorities that Adolf Hitler and Eva Braun had died by their own hands in the Fuehrer's private bunker in Berlin on April 30, a few hours after a macabre wedding feast.

Intelligence officers who have questioned almost a score of important witnesses and sifted all the available evidence are as convinced as they can he, lacking the actual bodies, that Hitler and his mistress killed themselves. The spokesman was almost as certain that Martin Bormann, Hitler's still uncaptured deputy, was killed while trying to escape from the bunker with the last defenders on the day after Hitler had died. However, while the evidence was sufficient to convince the British, the Russians are still as skeptical as ever.

Why they should retain such strong doubts the investigator did not know. But the British, he added, have not completed their investigation or called off the search.

SAY WOMAN MADE HIM STAY

The evidence indicated that, had it not been for his mistress' influence — she had her heart set on the reflected glory of dying with him in Berlin — Hitler might have followed his original plan of fleeing with his generals for a last stand in Bavaria. But he resisted all importunities to flee and went methodically about the business of self-destruction, arranging at his marriage feast for the slaughter of his pet Alsatian dog and making preparations to have his own and his bride's body burned. The conversation in his suite of the bunker during the wedding feast became so oppressive and morbid that, his secretary told the investigators, she could not stand it and excused herself early.

From April 22 until April 30, life in the bunker was pretty hectic. Hitler suffered periodic tantrums, charging and discovering new and old treacheries. He planned originally to leave for Berchtesgaden on April 20. At a staff meeting on April 22 he made it clear that he thought that the jig was up and he intended to remain in Berlin. Various people urged him to reconsider, but he heeded none.

On that day he had a nervous collapse. From that time on, his physical health was poor, but his mind seemed clear to his associates and he seemed even to achieve a relative calmness of spirit and an increased confidence in the outcome of the battle. Albert Speer, Minister of Armaments, visited him on the night of April 23 and heard in detail how Hitler planned to kill himself and have his body destroyed.

MARRIED ON APRIL 29

By April 29 the absurdity of hoping for the relief of Berlin was borne in even on Hitler. That night he married his mistress. After the marriage feast Hitler shook hands with his old retainers and said good-bye to them. This was about 2:30 A. M. on April 30. Some 12 hours later the transport office received orders to deliver 200 liters of gasoline to the Chancellery. At about that time Hitler and his bride again took leave of their faithful followers. It was the last time when they were seen alive.

Each then retired to his own apartment. Hitler shot himself through the mouth. Eva Braun, although she had a pistol, chose poison. A little later the two bodies were carried into the garden. Propaganda Minister Joseph Goebbels and Bormann acted as pall-bearers. Hitler's body was wrapped in a blanket.

Both bodies were soaked with gasoline, which the sandy soil of the garden absorbed, and, in the experts' view, gave forth as effluvia that consumed all but the bone structure of the bodies. These have been reduced to a state in which they were little more than dust and ashes, easily disposed of in a shallow grave that could be dug easily in the spacious garden.

Bormann, according to the witnesses, was killed leading the desperate garrison of the Chancellery in an attempt to escape through the Berlin subway. The tank beside which he was walking exploded crossing a bridge across the Spree River against Russian artillery fire.

Nazi Death Factory Shocks Germans on a Forced Tour

BY GENE CURRIVAN | APRIL 18, 1945

BUCHENWALD, GERMANY, APRIL 16 (DELAYED) — German civilians — 1,200 of them — were brought from the neighboring city of Weimar today to see for themselves the horror, brutality and human indecency perpetrated against their "neighbors" at the infamous Buchenwald concentration camp. They saw sights that brought tears to their eyes, and scores of them, including German nurses, just fainted away. They saw more than 20,000 nondescript prisoners, many of them barely living, who were all that remained of the normal complement of 80,000. The Germans were able to evacuate the others before we overran the place on April 10.

There were 32,705 that the "visiting" Germans didn't see, although they saw some of their bodies. It was this number that had been murdered since the camp was established in July, 1937. There was a time when the population reached more than 110,000, but the average was always below that. It included doctors, professors, scientists, statesmen, army officers, diplomats and an assortment of peasants and merchants from all over Europe and Asia.

There was a group of British officers among those left behind and one of seven French generals, but this was obviously an oversight in the great confusion that followed the news of our approach.

Five generals died and one escaped. This government-controlled camp was considered second only to that at Dachau, near Munich, as the world's worst atrocity center.

CRUELTY RAISED TO AN ART

It had its gallows, torture rooms, dissection rooms, modern crematoria, laboratories where fiendish experiments were made on living human beings and its sections where people were systematically starved to death.

This correspondent made a tour of the camp today and saw everything herein described. The statistics and an account of the events that happened before our troops liberated the camp were obtained from a special committee of prisoners, some of whom had been in the camp since its inception and others who had been German prisoners for twelve years. Their information was documented and in most cases confirmed by the records.

This story has already been told in part, but not until today has the full import of the atrocities been completely felt.

One of the first things that the German civilian visitors saw as they passed through the gates and into the interior of the camp was a display of "parchment." This consisted of large pieces of human flesh on which were elaborate tattooed markings. These strips had been collected by a German doctor who was writing a treatise on tattoos, and also by the 28-year-old wife of the Standartenfuehrer, or commanding officer. This woman, according to prisoners, was an energetic sportswoman who, back in Brandenburg, used to ride to hounds. She had a mania for unusual tattoos, and whenever a prisoner arrived who had a rare marking on his body, she would indicate that that trophy would make a valuable addition to her collection.

In addition to the "parchments" were two large table lamps, with parchment shades also made of human flesh.

The German people saw all this today, and they wept. Those who didn't weep were ashamed. They said they didn't know about it, and maybe they didn't, because the camp was restricted to Army personnel, but there it was right at their back doors for eight years.

The visitors stood in lines, one group at a time passing by the table on which the exhibits were displayed. A German-speaking American sergeant explained from an adjacent jeep what they were witnessing, while all around them were thousands of liberated "slaves" just looking on. Even the barracks roof was crowded with them. They watched silently. Some of them looked as if they were about to die, but this assemblage of "slaves" constituted the more healthy elements of the camp.

In barracks farther down the line were 3,000 sick who could not move and 4,800 aged who were unable to leave their squalid quarters. In addition, there were untold hundreds just roaming around, not knowing where they were or what was going on.

There were human skeletons who had lost all likeness to anything human. Most of them had become idiots, but they still had the power of locomotion. Those in the sick bay were beyond all help. They were packed into three-tier bunks, which ran to the roof of the barnlike barracks. They were dying there and no one could do anything about it.

The German visitors were to see them, too — and much more — but at the moment they were merely seeing "Exhibit A" and fainting.

Some Germans were skeptical at first as if this show had been staged for their benefit, but they were soon convinced. Even as they had milled along from one place to another, their own countrymen, who had been prisoners there, told them the story. Men went white and women turned away. It was too much for them.

GERMAN 'SCIENCE' EXHIBITED

These persons, who had been fed on Nazi propaganda since 1933, were beginning to see the light. They were seeing with their own eyes what no quantity of American propaganda could convince them of. Here was what their own government had perpetrated.

But they hadn't seen anything yet. In a barracks building in front of them was a scientific laboratory where captured scientists worked with material supplied by their overlords. There were shelves of bottles filled with various organs of the human body. In one was half a human head. It had been cut longitudinally to show all its component parts. This head once belonged to a prisoner, as did all the other human parts so displayed. In another room were a dozen death masks, skulls and shrunken human heads. A Czechoslovak scientist and surgeon who worked in the laboratory told us the history of each part, each head, each mask — because he had known the human beings to which they belonged. Some had been his own countrymen.

The German visitors saw this, too.

And then they were taken to another laboratory, where victims had been injected with typhus so that Germany could have typhus serum. There were still a score of "patients" who were still alive although the Polish doctor left behind, who had been forced to give these injections even to his own people, said the death rate had been 98 percent.

CHILDREN POISONED, TOO

This sight was too much for many German housewives, especially a little farther on, where only the children were kept. One 9-year-old boy, who had had only the first few injections, seemed quite chipper. He was Andor Gutman, a Hungarian Jew of Budapest. He had been in the camp three years. When asked where his parents were, he replied, without any emotion, "My father was killed and my mother was burned to death."

As one watched the Germans filing out of this building there was hardly a dry eye, although some tried to maintain their composure. There was real horror ahead, but some of them just couldn't go on.

From there they were taken to the living quarters. The stench, filth and misery here defied description. Those human wrecks standing in the corridor were beyond the stage where any amount of hospitalization could restore them to normal, while others peering helplessly from their bunks would be fortunate when they died.

There was a still lower grade in another barracks, where the prisoners were alive but could not rouse themselves. They were living skeletons. This was Barracks 58, and it was from here that they were taken to the crematory. This was the end of the road, and for them it was probably a godsend. The Germans saw this, too — and there was more to come.

The next exhibit was the most ghastly of all, although it was merely the disposal of the dead.

WELL-APPOINTED CREMATORY

In a little one-story red brick building, with a red tile roof, was a crematory with the most modern ovens that science can provide. But before you enter, you see a trailer stacked high with withered, starved, naked bodies. A few moments ago you saw the same thing, but those still had life in them. On top of the pile was a big robust body, fully clothed. This one had been murdered brutally.

Next to him was the body of an SS guard who had hanged himself on the day of our arrival. Former prisoners who had felt the lash of his whip cheerfully pointed out his body, and it was easy to identify because it had one stump leg.

In the crematory itself were two batteries of three ovens, each prominently marked with the makers' name — J. A. Topf & Sohne, Erfurt. This concern customarily manufactured baking ovens. These ovens were of extremely modern design and heated by coke. Narrow-gauge trucks were built into the concrete floor, and over these traveled steel contrivances resembling stretchers. Each oven had the remains of at least two bodies that had not yet been sifted into the chamber below. On a table near by were urns for the ashes. They looked like flower pots and were packed within metal containers, which, in turn, were packed in cardboard boxes for shipment to relatives. The names on the boxes, however, indicated that only Germans' remains were shipped.

Diminishing columns of German civilians also saw this. Then they were taken to the rear of the building where there was a gallows equipped for hanging five persons at a time. Just beyond was a pile of ashes from the furnaces.

The basement of the building was a torture chamber, where victims were forced to stand on low chairs, place a rope through a ring high on the wall and fasten the noose around their necks. The next victim got the job of kicking the chair from under them.

The next exhibit was the dissection room, adjacent to the crematory. This was a small, well-equipped cubicle with a white tile operating table and cabinets filled with surgical instruments. On hooks were several rubber aprons, and on the floor piles of prisoners' clothing. This was the room where the original owners of the "parchments" had been stripped of their skin.

The first prisoners to arrive at this camp were from Sachsenburg and Lichtenburg. In May and June of 1938, during the Gestapo wave of terror, the death rate was 10 percent. After von Rath was shot in Paris, 12,500 Jews were transported to Buchenwald.

In September 1939, arrivals at the camp included 2,500 Jews from old people's homes in Vienna. The following month 2,900 more arrived.

After the attempted assassination of Hitler, 21 Jews were selected arbitrarily and shot to death. All other Jews were kept in darkness for three days without food, and several days later the entire camp was deprived of food for five days.

AUXILIARY DEATH CAMPS USED

Before Buchenwald obtained its elaborate crematories prisoners who no longer could work were sent to Auschwitz to die or be killed in gas chambers. Auschwitz also had great furnaces. Reliable statements claim that 5,000 were disposed of there in three days. It as also at Auschwitz that Jewish women among the 30,000 once here at Buchenwald were sent to be exterminated after they had become pregnant. "Aryan" women in this group who were in similar physical condition were sent to Ravensbruck to have their children.

Buchenwald was bombed from the air on August 24 of last year because it was the site of a V-2 plant, which was just outside the main gates of the camp. It was here that many prisoners worked. The Nazis claimed that this bombing was the excuse for the murder of the German Communist party leader Ernst Thaelmann, but records show that Thaelmann was never in the camp.

The camp was liberated April 10 by the Eightieth Division. Two days later, President Roosevelt died, and the liberated prisoners unfurled a large black flag over the building at the entrance way. It still flies as a memorial to his death and to the dead within the camp. Those still living realize what he tried to do, and they doff their caps every time they see an American uniform.

As the sun went down tonight, and its last glow gave a softer touch to this distorted scene, which, paradoxically, is in a magnificent setting on a hilltop overlooking a valley, the German visitors were taken back to their homes. If they still think that Hitler and what he stands for is supreme, then we have lost the war. But observations made by this correspondent indicate that they are chastened people who have suffered today, but who will benefit by reflection in the long run.

Hitler Legends

BY W. E. FARBSTEIN | MAY 1, 1949

FOUR YEARS AGO today, the German Admiral Karl Doenitz gave the German people the news on the radio that Adolf Hitler "had met a hero's death at his post" in the Reich Chancellery in Berlin. But — heroic or not — had he?

Rumors that Hitler was still alive sprang up quickly. The Russian Marshal Zhukov, on June 9, 1945, declared that the Fuehrer in the last days of April "had married Eva Braun and perhaps escaped from Berlin by air."

The following November, the Allied Control Council formally reported that Hitler had died, and placed the time as "shortly after 2:30 P. M. on April 30, 1945." But that didn't stop the rumors. Many are still current, and new ones turn up frequently. Here are some of them.

Around Germany. Within a year after the war, a half dozen men claiming to be Adolf Hitler and as many women claiming to be Eva Braun turned up throughout the country. All were examined by physicians and sent to mental hospitals.

In Cologne. Police recently arrested a man who was distributing Hitler pamphlets in the city's main railway station. The brochures carried a swastika on the cover, and declared: "Our Fuehrer lives, and will return soon with unheard-of power. Oppose our persecutors and wait. Heil Hitler!" The man said he was paid for his work by "a foreign woman."

In Turin. A spiritualist medium named Giovanni Bocasso reported to the press that he had just had a psychic long-distance chat with Adolf Hitler, then residing on a tiny Polynesian isle. Eva Braun, the medium declared, was not with the Fuehrer, whose only companion is a French doctor.

In Stockholm. A Swedish newspaper reported that a former German Air Force captain named Baumgardt stated that he had flown Adolf Hitler and Eva Braun from Berlin to Denmark on April 26, 1945.

In Paris. A French traveling man named Max Gallon informed the newspapers that he had seen Adolf Hitler, healthy and cheerful, in the Tyrol. (M. Gallon was reputed to have worked closely with the Gestapo before the war.)

In Stuttgart. A former lieutenant colonel in the Elite Guard of the German Army declared that he had heard Adolf Hitler speaking from a mysterious radio station. Hitler had exhorted his followers to rise to power again, informing them that he had dozens of atomic bombs in readiness.

In Copenhagen. A newspaper reported the finding of a Hitler message in a bottle. It stated that Adolf Hitler had not died in Berlin, but on board a U-boat, which sank on Nov. 15, 1945, after colliding with a derelict.

In Rome. A Neapolitan soothsayer named d'Angelo declared that Adolf Hitler was not dead. Spiritual sources had informed him that Hitler was now living in a small town in western Argentina, to which he escaped by submarine from Denmark. The Fuehrer, the soothsayer added, was the guest of an Argentine millionaire, and there were four men and a woman in his party.

In Warsaw. A German SS pilot declared that Adolf Hitler and Eva Braun had fled to the United States aboard a submarine a few days before the fall of Berlin.

In Stockholm. A news service reported discovering evidence that a German grocer, resembling Hitler and carefully coached for the part, had been sent to Berlin to die in the Fuehrer's place.

In Wiesbaden. A refugee from Silesia stated that she had been living next door to Hitler and Eva Braun in the town of Liegnitz. "Hitler now has sideburns and a triangular mustache," she said, "and is living with a small, dark woman."

Hitler Reappraised, Ten Years Later

BY MAJ. H. R. TREVOR-ROPER | SEPT. 4, 1949

LONDON — It is now 10 years since Hitler, by invading Poland, declared war on the world. It was the climax of his career.

It had long been prepared, and carefully timed. "We are left with the decision," he had said in May, "to attack Poland at the first suitable opportunity." Now wag the opportunity. "I shall give a propagandist reason for starting the war," he had said in August. "Never mind whether it be plausible or not. After victory, no one will ask us whether we told the truth or not."

He knew that it meant war with the West: "The Polish conflict," he said, "is inseparable from conflict with the West"; but that did not deter him, he was so sure of victory.

"I am only afraid that at the last minute some *Schweinehund* will propose mediation."

Never was a war so cynically launched, with such full knowledge of its implications. The men of 1914 are accused of "blundering into war." Hitler is free from this imputation. His blunder was not in supposing that he could avoid war, but in being so confident of winning it.

Had Hitler won the war, his reputation would have seemed firm forever. As he said, people do not question the victors — at least in Germany. Since he failed, ruining his country, he has been denounced as a spirit of evil or decried as a mere mountebank. And yet, at one time he came very near to victory, is it fair that such extremes of reputation should depend on so narrow a difference? Anniversaries are useful occasions for reconsidering such matters.

Let us use the tenth anniversary of the war to reconsider the historical position of the man who made it. Was he a great man robbed by an accident of the success he deserved, or was he a charlatan, a lunatic whose lunacy, through an accident of time and place, happened to coincide with the spirit of an age, the ambitions of a whole people?

We have plenty of new evidence for such a reconsideration. Before the war we had, indeed, "Mein Kampf" (with its most significant parts expurgated from foreign translations), and we had Hermann Rauschning's record of Hitler's conversations, which were widely disbelieved, but which are now recognized as authentic. Otherwise we had only the public utterances of men who admitted that they believed in lying.

Now we have all the Nuremberg documents, including the official records of Hitler's conferences and conversations, his secret speeches and repeated "political testaments"; we have the diaries and affidavits of his intimates (like Goebbels) and his well-placed enemies (like Ulrich von Hassell); and we have that astonishing series of letters which he wrote to his former master, his bewitched satellite, Mussolini.

Finally, we have the knowledge of the events through which we have lived; perhaps the most powerful of all commentaries. What conclusions can we draw from this avalanche of new evidence, only now subsiding?

I do not believe that Hitler was a mere charlatan. It is true he had many of the qualities of a successful confidence trickster. He undoubtedly had a power of personal fascination, almost hypnosis, which drew crowds and inspired disciples. There is plenty of evidence of this. "It came over me in a vision," Rudolf Hess told his English captors, "that this man would lead Germany to greatness." "I saw this man," said Julius Streicher in the dock at Nuremberg, "after three hours of speaking, drenched in perspiration, and my neighbor thought he saw a halo round his head."

Goebbels, who could be skeptical enough at a distance, returned uncritical and inspired from the Fuehrer's presence. Even Speer, the sanest of his court, admitted that Hitler's eyes drained him of vitality. And yet, if this gift is common in crooks, lunatics and religious revivalists, which of them had used it to such effect as he did? Hitler may have had some of the qualities of a bogus California swami, but it was not with these that he upset the whole world.

Whatever else may be said of him, Hitler had certain real marks of mental greatness. He was a great systematizer, a simplifier of genius. He saw the central problem of Europe, within his own experience, and within his own intellectual limitations he devised a solution for it. It was a solution detestable to every liberal and humane person, but at least it was a possible solution, logical and practical.

Further, he could present his solution in such simple terms and with such confidence that millions of people thought that they understood it, and accepted it as a talisman that would cure the world. Finally, the clarity and the narrowness of his vision enabled him to concentrate upon the fulfillment of a terrible program all the extraordinary energy of his mind.

What was the problem which Hitler saw? He saw that the industrialization of Europe had created a new proletariat, subject to new dangers, new passions and prejudices, capable of subverting the known world, but capable also of being exploited. He saw that the collapse of the Central Powers in 1918, and its economic consequences, had threatened the living standards both of the workers and of the middle classes, and turned both the docile slaves and the front-line supporters of society into frightened mutineers.

Throughout Central Europe society was precarious, and no patching and tinkering, no conventions or expedients seemed able to shore it up. The old ruling classes could not solve this problem, because their privileges exempted them from it; the middle classes were too timid to face it; the Socialists were useless, for they misunderstood the psychology of the masses. The victorious powers would give no real help. Why should they? Equal treatment would be a denial of victory and would only extend the problem to themselves. What, then, was the answer? The problem seemed insoluble.

Hitler declared that it was not — at least not for Germany. The answer, he declared, was not to cure slavery but to shift its incidence: to destroy the old privileged classes, now obsolete; to reverse the verdict of 1918, and the privileges of the victors; to organize and realize the power of the illiterate masses; and then, artificial privileges being swept away, the laws of nature could assert themselves: the race would be to the strong, the Germans would be the masters, the rest of Europe the slaves.

Were not the Germans the most numerous, the most industrious national unit in Europe? Then economically and numerically they could dominate it. Had they not the greatest military tradition in the world? Then militarily they could hold it down. Geographically central, they seemed by the laws of geopolitics to destine for such a future. The present balance of power was artificial — the cost of maintaining it prohibitive. But once the natural balance had been restored, then the natural rulers, the *Herrenvolk*, would maintain themselves cheaply in power forever. The nightmare of unemployment, fear and degradation would have been shifted on to those lesser peoples whose resentment would be too weak to disconcert the natural balance. The problem — for Germany — would be solved.

How luminous it seemed, but how impossible! Germany was defeated, disarmed, dispossessed. Such a change was inconceivable. Hitler rejected such defeatism. Nothing, he said, was impossible, given confidence and a man of genius like himself. There had been great changes in previous history. How had they been attained? Not by argument, not by objective justice, humanity or superior culture. The barbarians had been less civilized than the Romans, the Romans than the Etruscans, Greeks, Levantines. Carthage had not been conciliated, but crushed. Force and fraud, ruthlessness and vandalism, a bloodthirsty religion and bestial fanaticism — these were the means whereby great historical changes had been effected, and could be effected again. Culture (he wrote in "Mein Kampf") could develop later.

All Hitler's life was devoted to achieving this change by these means. The program was huge and detailed. It entailed vast preparation, immense skill and patience, infinite craft and careful organization. It entailed temporary appeasement of certain classes, certain nations. But since it also entailed the extrusion from Europe of Britain, the reduction of France and the total conquest of Russia, it would certainly also entail a major war.

By skillful diplomacy, by ruthless deceit, the scope and risks of the war might be reduced; but ultimately it would have to be fought. For that he needed in reserve a fanatical idea. Since no one would gain from victory except Germans, he did not need any universal idea, although incidental baits might lure casual allies: For the essential struggle, mere Germanism was enough; but it must be quite uncompromising. It did not matter if it was absurd — fanatics never notice their absurdities. So he dipped his pitcher into the deep black well of German nationalism, coated with ancient slime and full of strange creatures, and drew up the horrible draught of nazism to intoxicate his myrmidons.

Now that so many documents have become available, we can see how completely Hitler saw himself as the architect of a new historical era, the Demiurge who alone was strong enough to perform the miracle of change. He described himself in "Mein Kampf" as the genius who appeared "at long intervals of human history." "It often seems to me," he wrote to Mussolini 20 years later, "that human development has only been interrupted for fifteen hundred years and is now about to resume its former character"; and he harked back as always to his "Golden Age" — the Persian and Punic Wars, the invasion of the Huns and Mongols.

Convinced that only he could achieve this miracle, Hitler was terrified by the thought that death might prevent him or the timidity of others delay him in his task. "Essentially it all depends on me, on my existence," he told his admirals and generals in May, 1939. "There will probably never again be a man with power such as mine ... but I can be eliminated at any time by a criminal or an idiot." "I know, O Duce," he wrote to Mussolini, "how difficult it is to take historic decisions. I do not think that after my death any other man will be strong enough for the task." "If anyone should say that our tasks can be left to a future generation," he announced at a diplomatic conference, "I reply that the future may not produce a generation of giants. The resurrection of

Germany took thirty years. Rome never rose again. This is the voice of history."

Clearly, Hitler saw his historical function as a Wagnerian grand opera. Vast cosmic changes required an accompaniment of slaughter on a colossal scale. He did not flinch from this — he was "the hardest man in centuries" — indeed, he enjoyed it. There is evidence that Hitler derived a positive aesthetic satisfaction from the thought of slaughter, of wholesale massacres and rivers of blood. When he looked for a parallel, he looked to the barbarians who conquered Rome and, particularly, to the Mongol conqueror, Genghis Khan. The history of Genghis Khan was a compulsory subject of study in the SS. In Asia Genghis Khan is reported to have slaughtered 18,000,000 men, 2,000,000 in the city of Herat alone. Otherwise he achieved nothing of importance.

All this is clearly megalomania, but it cannot be written off as mere megalomania. What distinguished Hitler's megalomania was the extraordinary concentration of skill, organization and will-power which nearly made it a success; the new techniques of power, new forms of warfare, new methods of propaganda and diplomacy, which he devised and carried out. It is impossible to read "Mein Kampf," or the record of his conversations and conferences without observing — among the turgid and repetitive bombast, the brutal sadism and disgusting nationalism — the streaks of genius and intuition, the clear and terrible realism, the luminous simplification of vast problems into a sudden relevant truth. These are evidence not of a mania but of genius.

And yet, in human terms, how squalid a genius he was! Vulgar minds worship mere power and there will always be people who will admire Hitler simply for the exorbitance of his ambition and the narrowness of his failure, without regard to its human purpose and cost. Hitler himself had such in mind and (after Genghis Khan) reserved his admiration for Stalin simply because he had achieved greater power and eliminated more opponents than himself. Mussolini, he said, was an altogether inferior character, for he had not yet destroyed the monarchy or the church and hesitated to murder his relations.

More critical people ask other questions. They ask what kind of man Hitler was outside politics; and even inside politics they may consider that political programs have some relevance to human happiness. One admits such thoughts and the stature of Hitler shrinks to contemptible size.

First, his personality outside of politics. If we compare Hitler as a man with those others who, like him, seem to have discovered the master key to revolutionary politics — with Napoleon or Lenin — at once an abyss seems to open between them. It is not merely that they were men of superior culture. By the standards of his time, Napoleon was not, and his contemporaries felt toward him the same contempt which educated Germans felt for Hitler, with his violent tantrums and lower middle-class tastes.

But these are class judgments which genius transcends. Where Hitler and Napoleon or Lenin really differ is not in taste but in mental quality.

"A great man," says Norman Douglas, speaking of Napoleon's care for such details as forest policy in Italy, "will leave his mark on minutiae." Similarly, Oliver Cromwell, amid all the preoccupations of power, would intervene in a hundred obscure local matters and everywhere these little interventions, even when his enemies record them, have an authentic touch of greatness, of Olympian humanity.

Hitler had no such range of greatness. His dark, contorted genius might sometimes flash out as it wrestled with problems of revolution and war; but in ordinary affairs, in casual conversation, in the world of humanity and ideas, we look in vain for any symptom of illumination or magnanimity. We find only a coarse and banal mind or listen to a dreary tedious bore. Table talk of really great men is worth collecting. Hitler's is not. Outside of revolutionary politics it consists of ranting superlatives made disgusting by inhumanity.

Even inside politics. Hitler's genius was equally arid and inhuman. All other great revolutionary leaders have achieved success by exploiting an idea. It has not always been a nice idea; it has generally been debased by public currency and has generated cant and nonsense around it. But fundamentally there has been a real idea which, in its purest form, has been capable of moving men and starting in the intellectual world an avalanche of further thought. We may not like Marxism. In its present Stalinist form we may consider it obscurantist and reactionary nonsense, but in its history it has enriched the intellectual world and it is impossible even for its strongest opponents to think as they would if it had never been.

Napoleon also exploited an idea which has also been a fertilizing intellectual influence. Further, the ideas both of the French and Russian revolutions were, or could be, humane ideas they had a generous content which appealed to the humanity of the world and was welcomed (therein lay their explosive quality) far beyond national frontiers. Napoleon's conquering army was greeted, at least in its early days, as the bearer of new hope to foreign lands; and communism, until its consequences became obvious, held out similar promises to exploited workers of every country.

Hitler had no such idea. To him the purpose of politics was not intellectual advancement, social improvement or human happiness; it was simply the pursuit, through artificially revived barbarism, of mere power. In human beings he had no interest at all; they were simply the material of polity. He despised all men, and Germans (for whose welfare he sometimes claimed that he was destroying the rest of the world) he despised most of all. They were "a race of sheep," and "unworthy of his great ideas"; and when they refused to be sacrificed on the altar of his power, he stated openly that they deserved to perish.

Throughout his career, though he might fascinate individuals and hypnotize crowds, Hitler never sought personal contact with his people. He never mixed with crowds. When he visited the front he was hurried in secrecy from airport to headquarters; he never in his life visited a bombed city. Had he succeeded in his ambitions he would have rewarded the Germans with a higher standard of living; but he offered it with gestures of contempt as the compensation of slavery.

Having failed, Hitler's sterile gospel can interest nobody. It had no pure form, no generous content. No new currents of thought or art could spring from such a source. Napoleonism, thanks to some of its implications, lingered on in Germany, in Italy and in Poland long after Napoleon had failed. In liberated Europe who regrets Hitler?

This then, is my verdict on Hitler in history. If we consider him as a German revolutionary politician, we must admit him, however reluctantly, as one of the great geniuses of our time: He found, as men seldom find, the key of a century and worked thereby a miracle of success and conquest. It is impossible to think or moralize him into insignificance.

But German revolutionary politics are not everything. If quality, as distinct from mere scope and size, means anything in human affairs, Hitler was a contemptible figure. His mind had great power, but no touch of quality; it was coarse and trivial. He was the least magnanimous conqueror in modern history. He was right to compare himself not with Napoleon or Lenin, but with Attila and Genghis Khan.

H. R. TREVOR-ROPER, A HISTORY DON AT OXFORD, BECAME AN AUTHORITY ON HITLER WHEN HE WAS OFFICIALLY ASSIGNED BY HIS GOVERNMENT TO INVESTIGATE THE FUEHRER'S DEATH AFTER THE WAR. HE IS THE AUTHOR OF THE BOOK "THE LAST DAYS OF HITLER."

Hitler — 25 Years Ago Today

BY THE NEW YORK TIMES | JAN. 30, 1958

A THUNDEROUS QUARTER of a century ago today, on Jan. 30, 1933, a hitherto insignificant and even comical figure going by the name of Adolf Hitler came to power in Germany — and stayed in power long enough to set the world aflame. It was on that fateful day that a deluded German President, a beguiled German people and a cowardly party coalition permitted him to become Chancellor and then abdicated all power, all reason, all self-respect and all morality to what turned out to be a madman.

Though he had already demonstrated his hypnotic influence by organizing a mass movement and revealed his ruthlessness by the strong-arm methods of his private army, his rise was largely due to consistent underestimation of him at home and abroad. The old German leadership elite in particular, including politicians, generals and businessmen, all thought that he would "calm down" with responsibility and that in any case they would be able to "handle" him. That enabled him to come to power legally in order, as his Propaganda Minister Goebbels said, to act illegally afterward. He was, of course, aided by the great depression which had made millions unemployed and had raised the specter of bolshevism that frightened many Germans into seeking safety in the opposite extreme. But his "legal revolution," now being tried by the Soviets in other countries, was one contribution to political methodology.

He ended 12 years later as a cornered fugitive from world justice by shooting himself. But in these 12 years he had precipitated the greatest holocaust in history. His armies conquered most of Europe, but in the end made a shambles of both Germany and the rest of the continent and brought Soviet power to the heart of Europe. The world is still trying to extricate itself from the evil Hitler wrought, and it is gratifying that the new Germany of Chancellor Adenauer is among the leaders in that effort.

Glossary

Arminius Germanic tribal chief of the 1st century BCE and 1st century CE who led a successful ambush against the attacking Roman legions led by General Varus in the Battle of the Teutoburg Forest.

bolshevism Russian doctrine of communism practiced by the Bolsheviks promoting the violent overthrow of capitalism.

brassard A cloth band worn around the upper arm displaying a symbol or mark.

burgher A member of the middle class.

coadjutor One who shares an office or assists another with a position.

cuirassier Armed cavalry, especially those who fought for France in the Napoleonic Wars.

desperado An outlaw.

Falangista Members of the Spanish General Francisco Franco's far-right fascist political party, the Falange Española.

Fascisti Members of a fascist political party, especially Italian prime minister Benito Mussolini's National Fascist Party.

franctireur A guerrilla fighter.

fulmination A denunciation or censure.

Furor Teutonicus Latin phrase referring to the perceived ferocity of the Germanic tribes during the period of the Roman Empire.

gauleiter The title of a district leader in Nazi Germany.

Gestapo The secret state police of the Nazi regime.

Hakenkreuz German name of the swastika, the symbol of the Nazi party.

harangue To lecture with an aggressive, critical tone.

Herr German title equivalent to the English "Mr."

histrionic Overly dramatic or theratrical.

inchoate Not yet fully developed or formed.

Junker A member of the Prussian nobility.

neurasthenia Psychiatric diagnosis often used in the late 19th and early 20th centuries for patients exhibiting fatigue, high blood pressure, anxiety, and depression, among other symptoms.

Orgesch An anti-Semitic paramilitary organization founded by German politician Georg Escherich in 1920 and disbanded shortly thereafter.

parley A discussion with enemies to establish a truce or similar matter.

plunderbund An agreement or association of political, financial or commercial interests that exploit the public.

putsch A secretly plotted attempt to overthrow the government.

Reichstag The German legislative body.

Reichswehr The German military organization from 1919 to 1935.

rescript An official announcement or decree.

truncheon A baton or bludgeon.

usurer One who lends money at a high-interest rate.

Media Literacy Terms

"Media literacy" refers to the ability to access, understand, critically assess and create media. The following terms are important components of media literacy, and they will help you critically engage with the articles in this title.

angle The aspect of a news story that a journalist focuses on and develops.

attribution The method by which a source is identified or by which facts and information are assigned to the person who provided them.

balance Principle of journalism that both perspectives of an argument should be presented in a fair way.

bias A disposition in favor of a certain idea, person or perspective.

byline Name of the writer, usually placed between the headline and the story.

chronological order Method of writing a story presenting the details of the story in the order in which they occurred.

credibility The quality of being trustworthy and believable, said of a journalistic source.

editorial Article of opinion or interpretation.

feature story Article designed to entertain as well as to inform.

headline Type, usually 18 point or larger, used to introduce a story.

human interest story Type of story that focuses on individuals and how events or issues affect their life, generally offering a sense of relatability to the reader.

impartiality Principle of journalism that a story should not reflect a journalist's bias and should contain balance.

intention The motive or reason behind something, such as the publication of a news story.

interview story Type of story in which the facts are gathered primarily by interviewing another person or persons.

inverted pyramid Method of writing a story using facts in order of importance, beginning with a lead and then gradually adding paragraphs in order of relevance from most interesting to least interesting.

motive The reason behind something, such as the publication of a news story or a source's perspective on an issue.

news story An article or style of expository writing that reports news, generally in a straightforward fashion and without editorial comment.

op-ed An opinion piece that reflects a prominent journalist's opinion on a topic of interest.

paraphrase The summary of an individual's words, with attribution, rather than a direct quotation of their exact words.

quotation The use of an individual's exact words indicated by the use of quotation marks and proper attribution.

reliability The quality of being dependable and accurate, said of a journalistic source.

rhetorical device Technique in writing intending to persuade the reader or communicate a message from a certain perspective.

tone A manner of expression in writing or speech.

Media Literacy Questions

1. In "New Popular Idol Rises in Bavaria" (on page 10), Cyril Brown directly quotes an unnamed informant. Why would Brown not name his source? How does anonymity impact the source's credibility?

2. What is the intention of Joseph Shaplen's article "Hitler, Driving Force in Germany's Fascism" (on page 27)? What rhetorical devices does Shaplen use? How do they help him achieve this intention?

3. What kind of story is "Hitler Endorsed by 9 to 1 in Poll on His Dictatorship, But Opposition Is Doubled" (on page 49)? What is the purpose of such a story?

4. What is the tone of Anne O'Hare McCormick's article "Hitler Is Already Creating New Wars of Tomorrow" (on page 81)? Is it similar in tone to her later article "The Ascent and Decline of Adolf Hitler" (on page 138)?

5. "Assurances from Hitler" (on page 114) offers a series of quoted pledges Hitler made followed by details of his actions to the contrary. What is the intention of the article? How does its structure help achieve that intent?

6. The article "Hitler Said to Lose Little Man's Faith" (on page 136) is an example of a human interest story. What is the purpose of a human interest story? How well does this article achieve that?

7. What is the intention of Edwin L. James's article "Hitler's Biggest

Lie" (on page 141)? What rhetorical devices does he use? Is he effective in achieving his intention?

8. What is the tone of the article "Hitler's Fifty-Five Years" (on page 161)? What do you think is the motive behind the article?

9. In Meyer Berger's article "City Takes Report of Death in Stride" (on page 175), Berger reports various New York residents' reaction to the news of Hitler's death. What is the article's tone? How do the quotations contribute to that tone?

10. Describe the structure of the article "Hitler Legends" by W. E. Farbstein (on page 198)? What is its tone? What do you think is the article's intention?

11. What kind of story is "Nazi Death Factory Shocks Germans on a Forced Tour" (on page 191)? What is the purpose of such a story?

Citations

All citations in this list are formatted according to the
Modern Language Association's (MLA) style guide.

BOOK CITATION

NEW YORK TIMES EDITORIAL STAFF, THE. *Adolf Hitler*. New York: New York
   Times Educational Publishing, 2019.

ARTICLE CITATIONS

AXELSSON, GEORGE. "Hitler Mystery Adds to Uneasy Reich's Woes." *The New
   York Times*, 19 Nov. 1944, https://www.nytimes.com/1944/11/19/archives/
   hitler-mystery-adds-to-uneasy-reichs-woes-filtering-of-rumors.html.

AXELSSON, GEORGE. "Hitler Said to Lose Little Man's Faith." *The New York
   Times*, 3 Dec. 1942, https://www.nytimes.com/1942/12/03/archives/hitler
   -said-to-lose-little-mans-faith-people-in-berlin-reported-to.html.

BERGER, MEYER. "City Takes Report of Death in Stride." *The New York Times*,
   2 May 1945, https://www.nytimes.com/1945/05/02/archives/city-takes
   -report-of-death-in-stride-as-the-report-of-hitlers-death.html.

BIRCHALL, FREDERICK T. "Hitler Endorsed by 9 to 1 in Poll on His Dictatorship,
   But Opposition is Doubled." *The New York Times*, 20 Aug. 1934, https://
   www.nytimes.com/1934/08/20/archives/hitler-endorsed-by-9-to-1-in-poll
   -on-his-dictatorship-but.html.

BROOKS PETERS, C. "Hitler Challenges World Democracy." *The New York
   Times*, 11 Dec. 1940, https://www.nytimes.com/1940/12/11/archives/hitler
   -challenges-world-democracy-holding-nazi-way-richer-he-says.html.

BROWN, CYRIL. "New Popular Idol Rises in Bavaria." *The New York Times*, 21
   Nov. 1922, https://www.nytimes.com/1922/11/21/archives/new-popular
   -idol-rises-in-bavaria-hitler-credited-with.html.

BROWN, WALTER. "Hitler's Real 'Kampf.' " *The New York Times*, 14 June 1942,

https://www.nytimes.com/1942/06/14/archives/hitlers-real-kampf-this
-summer-promises-to-bring-the-big-crisis-in.html.

CURRIVAN, GENE. "Nazi Death Factory Shocks Germans on a Forced Tour." *The New York Times*, 18 April 1945, https://www.nytimes.com/1945/04/18/archives/nazi-death-factory-shocks-germans-on-a-forced-tour-german-civilians.html.

DANIELL, RAYMOND. "Hitler Ended Life in Berlin Bunker, British Feel Sure." *The New York Times*, 2 May 1945, https://www.nytimes.com/1945/11/02/archives/hitler-ended-life-in-berlin-bunker-british-feel-sure-nazi-leader.html.

ENDERIS, GUIDO. "Fascists Make Big Gains in Germany." *The New York Times*, 15 Sept. 1930, https://www.nytimes.com/1930/09/15/archives/fascists-make-big-gains-in-germany-communists-also-increase.html.

ENDERIS, GUIDO. "Group Formed by Papen, Hitler Is Named Reich Chancellor." *The New York Times*, 31 Jan. 1933, https://www.nytimes.com/1933/01/31/archives/group-formed-by-papen-nationalists-to-dominate-in-government-led-by.html.

ENDERIS, GUIDO. "Rule Till 1937 Sought." *The New York Times*, 21 Mar. 1933, https://www.nytimes.com/1933/03/21/archives/rule-till-1937-sought-bill-bars-legislation-by-deputies-unless-they.html.

FARBSTEIN, W. E. "Hitler Legends." *The New York Times*, 1 May 1949, https://www.nytimes.com/1949/05/01/archives/hitler-legends.html.

GUEDALLA, PHILIP. "If Napoleon Couldn't, Can Hitler?" *The New York Times*, 2 Feb. 1941, https://www.nytimes.com/1941/02/02/archives/if-napoleon-couldnt-can-hitler-napoleon-and-hitler.html.

JAMES, EDWIN L. "Again Hitler Rewrites Vital Page of History." *The New York Times*, 1 Feb. 1942, https://www.nytimes.com/1942/02/01/archives/again-hitler-rewrites-vital-page-of-history-fuehrer-gives-roosevelt.html.

JAMES, EDWIN L. "Herr Hitler Rewrites Military Story of 1918." *The New York Times*, 23 June 1940, https://www.nytimes.com/1940/06/23/archives/herr-hitler-rewrites-military-story-of-1918-fuehrer-retells-his.html.

JAMES, EDWIN L. "Hitler's Biggest Lie." *The New York Times*, 11 Apr. 1943, https://www.nytimes.com/1943/04/11/archives/hitlers-biggest-lie-the-fuehrers-lies-are-legion-and-colossal-his.html.

KNAUTH, PERCIVAL. "Hitler Forswears 'Any Compromise.' " *The New York Times*, 9 Nov. 1940, https://www.nytimes.com/1940/11/09/archives/hitler-forswears-any-compromise-tells-nazi-old-guard-he-is.html.

KNAUTH, PERCIVAL. "Hitler Welcomed by Frenzied Berlin." *The New York*

Times, 7 July 1940, https://www.nytimes.com/1940/07/07/archives/hitler
-welcomed-by-frenzied-berlin-thousands-cheer-chancellor-on.html.

THE NEW YORK TIMES. "Assurances from Hitler." *The New York Times*, 2 Jan. 1941,
https://www.nytimes.com/1941/01/02/archives/assurances-from-hitler.html.

THE NEW YORK TIMES. "Bavarian Riots Continue." *The New York Times*, 12 Nov.
1923, https://www.nytimes.com/1923/11/12/archives/bavarian-riots
-continue-incensed-people-join-in-demonstrations.html.

THE NEW YORK TIMES. "Broken Promises Fill Hitler Record." *The New York
Times*, 2 May 1945, https://www.nytimes.com/1945/05/02/archives/broken
-promises-fill-hitler-record-pledges-repeatedly-flouted-as.html.

THE NEW YORK TIMES. "Fascists Glorify Pan-German Ideal." *The New York
Times*, 15 Sept. 1930, https://www.nytimes.com/1930/09/15/archives/
fascists-glorify-pangerman-ideal-stand-for-ultranationalism.html.

THE NEW YORK TIMES. "Foes Are Warned." *The New York Times*, 2 May 1939,
https://www.nytimes.com/1939/05/02/archives/foes-are-warned-fuehrer
-holds-we-would-do-better-to-take-his-goods.html.

THE NEW YORK TIMES. "Fuehrer Ascetic in Personal Life." *The New York Times*,
2 May 1945, https://www.nytimes.com/1945/05/02/archives/
fuehrer-ascetic-in-personal-life-celibate-and-a-vegetarian-he.html.

THE NEW YORK TIMES. "German Citizenship Acquired by Hitler." *The New York
Times*, 26 Feb. 1932, https://www.nytimes.com/1932/02/26/archives/
german-citizenship-acquired-by-hitler-he-receives-an-appointment-to.html.

THE NEW YORK TIMES. "He Only Wanted To Be Liked." *The New York Times*, 6
Sept. 1940, https://www.nytimes.com/1940/09/06/archives/he-only-wanted
-to-be-liked.html.

THE NEW YORK TIMES. "Hitler Bids Reich Die for Nazi Tenets." *The New York
Times*, 31 Jan. 1945, https://www.nytimes.com/1945/01/31/archives/hitler
-bids-reich-die-for-nazi-tenets-strives-to-kindle-hope-for.html.

THE NEW YORK TIMES. "Hitler Glorified at Nazi Art Show." *The New York
Times*, 17 July 1932, https://www.nytimes.com/1937/07/17/archives/hitler
-glorified-at-nazi-art-show-is-called-greatest-master-of.html.

THE NEW YORK TIMES. "Hitler Hails Ties with Italy, Japan." *The New York
Times*, 8 Sept. 1937, https://www.nytimes.com/1937/09/08/archives/hitler
-hails-ties-with-italy-japan-warns-community-of-will-between.html.

THE NEW YORK TIMES. "Hitler Is Insane, Specialist Holds." *The New York*

Times, 20 Oct. 1939, https://www.nytimes.com/1939/10/20/archives/hitler
-is-insane-specialist-holds-dr-brown-of-oxford-says-the.html.

THE NEW YORK TIMES. "Hitler Sees Fight to Finish in Reich." *The New York
Times*, 18 Jan. 1932, https://www.nytimes.com/1932/01/18/archives/hitler
-sees-fight-to-finish-in-reich-says-unity-cant-be-achieved-by.html.

THE NEW YORK TIMES. "Hitler — 25 Years Ago Today." *The New York Times*, 30 Jan.
1958, https://timesmachine.nytimes.com/timesmachine/1958/01/30/
79444601.html.

THE NEW YORK TIMES. "Hitler's Fifty-Five Years." *The New York Times*, 20 Apr. 1944,
https://www.nytimes.com/1944/04/20/archives/hitlers-fiftyfive-years.html.

THE NEW YORK TIMES. "Hitler's Home Guard." *The New York Times*, 19 Oct. 1944,
https://www.nytimes.com/1944/10/19/archives/hitlers-home-guard.html.

THE NEW YORK TIMES. "Hitler's Last Arguments." *The New York Times*, 31 Jan. 1944,
https://www.nytimes.com/1944/01/31/archives/hitlers-last-arguments.html.

THE NEW YORK TIMES. "Hitler's Last Kampf." *The New York Times*, 22 Sept. 1944,
https://www.nytimes.com/1944/09/22/archives/hitlers-last-kampf.html.

THE NEW YORK TIMES. "Hitler's Last Victories." *The New York Times*, 23 Mar. 1944,
https://www.nytimes.com/1944/03/23/archives/hitlers-last-victories.html.

THE NEW YORK TIMES. "Hitler's Last Weapon." *The New York Times*, 3 July 1944,
https://www.nytimes.com/1944/07/03/archives/hitlers-last-weapon.html.

THE NEW YORK TIMES. "Hitler's Rhetoric." *The New York Times*, 27 Sept. 1930,
https://www.nytimes.com/1930/09/27/archives/hitlers-rhetoric.html.

THE NEW YORK TIMES. "Hitler Tamed by Prison." *The New York Times*, 21
Dec. 1924, https://www.nytimes.com/1924/12/21/archives/hitler-tamed
-by-prison-released-on-parole-he-is-expected-to-return.html.

THE NEW YORK TIMES. "Hitler Tells the Reichstag 'Bomb Will Be Met by Bomb.' "
The New York Times, 21 Dec. 1924, https://www.nytimes.com/
1939/09/01/archives/hitler-tells-the-reichstag-bomb-will-be-met-by-bomb
-chancellor-vows.html.

THE NEW YORK TIMES. "Hitler Vows a Finish Fight, Warns Dissidents of Death." *The
New York Times*, 9 Nov. 1943, https://www.nytimes.com/1943/11/09/archives/
hitler-vows-a-finish-fight-warns-dissidents-of-death-hitler-vows.html.

THE NEW YORK TIMES. "Hitler Writes a Book While in Prison Cell." *The New York
Times*, 1 Sept. 1939, https://www.nytimes.com/1924/05/30/archives/hitler
-writes-a-book-while-in-prison-cell-tells-interviewer-his.html.

THE NEW YORK TIMES. "Nazis Rate Hitler a Military Genius." *The New York Times*, 21 Apr. 1940, https://www.nytimes.com/1940/04/21/archives/nazis-rate-hitler-a-military-genius-german-acclaim-to-him-on-his.html.

THE NEW YORK TIMES. "Rogue's Progress: 1933-1942." *The New York Times*, 30 Jan. 1942, https://www.nytimes.com/1942/01/30/archives/rogues-progress-19331942.html.

THE NEW YORK TIMES. "Seven Years of Hitler." *The New York Times*, 29 Jan. 1940, https://www.nytimes.com/1940/01/29/archives/seven-years-of-hitler.html.

THE NEW YORK TIMES. "The Last of Hitler." *The New York Times*, 7 June 1945, https://www.nytimes.com/1945/06/07/archives/the-last-of-hitler.html.

O'HARE MCCORMICK, ANNE. "Hitler Is Already Creating New Wars of Tomorrow." *The New York Times*, 18 Sept. 1939, https://www.nytimes.com/1939/09/18/archives/in-europe-hitler-is-already-creating-new-wars-of-tomorrow.html.

O'HARE MCCORMICK, ANNE. "The Ascent and Decline of Adolf Hitler." *The New York Times*, 30 Jan. 1943, https://www.nytimes.com/1943/01/30/archives/abroad-the-ascent-and-decline-of-adolf-hitler.html.

SHAPLEN, JOSEPH. "Hitler, Driving Force in Germany's Fascism." *The New York Times*, 21 Sept. 1930, https://www.nytimes.com/1930/09/21/archives/hitler-driving-force-in-germanys-fascism-his-fiery-oratory-has-won.html.

TOLISCHUS, OTTO D. "Nazis Pay Tribute: Millions in Berlin Hall Hail Hitler as Leader on His 50th Birthday." *The New York Times*, 21 Apr. 1939, http://www.nytimes.com/1939/04/21/archives/nazis-pay-tribute-millions-in-berlin-hail-hitler-as-leader-on-his.html.

TOLISCHUS, OTTO D. "Nazi World Revolution Is Hitler's Objective." *The New York Times*, 12 May 1940, https://www.nytimes.com/1940/05/12/archives/nazi-world-revolution-is-hitlers-objective-german-master-race-is.html.

TOLISCHUS, OTTO D. "President Backs Hitler." *The New York Times*, 3 July 1934, https://www.nytimes.com/1934/07/03/archives/president-backs-hitler-decision-is-held-to-have-been-made-because.html.

TOLISCHUS, OTTO D. "Reich Adopts Swastika as Nation's Official Flag, Anti-Jewish Laws Passed." *The New York Times*, 16 Sept. 1935, https://www.nytimes.com/1935/09/16/archives/reich-adopts-swastika-as-nations-official-flag-hitlers-reply-to.html.

TREVOR-ROPER, MAJ. H. R. "Hitler Reappraised, Ten Years Later." The New York Times, 4 Sept. 1949, https://www.nytimes.com/1949/09/04/archives/hitler-reappraised-ten-years-after-almost-a-conqueror-a.html.

Index